GRAVE
*fro*ı.
BERKSHIRE

*A unique guide to the county's
strange, striking and curious
epitaphs and memorials*

Diana Costin
Drawings: Barry Costin

S.B. Publications

First published in 1999 by S.B. Publications
c/o 19 Grove Road, Seaford, East Sussex, BN25 1TP

ISBN 1 85770 157 7

Typset by JEM Lewes
Printed by
MFP Design and Print
Stretford Manchester
M32 0JT

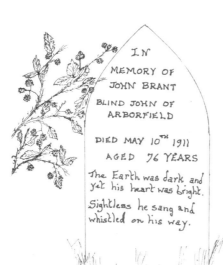

IN
MEMORY OF
JOHN BRANT
BLIND JOHN OF
ARBORFIELD

DIED MAY 10ᵀᴴ 1911
AGED 76 YEARS

The Earth was dark and
yet his heart was bright.
Sightless he sang and
whistled on his way.

St Bartholomew's, Aborfield.

CONTENTS

Front cover: Tibbs in the churchyard of St Matthew, Wallingford.
Back cover: The churchyard of St Michael, Sunninghill.

INTRODUCTION

P ASSING through the lychgate to wander among the gravestones is a
nourishing and serene experience for the soul. For three years I spent
many hours in churchyards researching for this book, and taking photographs,
and I enjoyed every minute of it. The result is a record of some of Berkshire's
more interesting gravestones, with just a few borrowed from the part of
Oxfordshire that used to be in old Berkshire.

What I discovered almost straight away is how popular churchyards are.
One or two were so hidden away, such as that at Speen, that I saw nobody,
others like St Nicholas at Hurst were quite busy. It was here that I spotted a
man dressed in a suit lying on the grass, next to a flat tombstone, fast asleep.
In other churchyards there were people sitting reading or just thinking, others
eating sandwiches, tending graves, walking the dog, wheeling a bicycle. A
couple in one place walked arm in arm among the gravestones, holding their
crash helmets. Wherever I went this was how churchyards were being used.

Many churches are now locked because of vandalism. Cemeteries and cre-
matoriums have gates that close at certain times every day, but churchyards,
for the living as well as the dead, are open all the time. They have always
been used by the whole community, not only to bury the dead, but for holding
markets, taking wedding photographs, grazing animals.

John Betjeman hated churchyard clearance and liked tombstones for their
own sake, so that he and other people could be reminded of the transience of
life. He believed that scythes and sheep were far better at dealing with the
grass than motor mowers. Some churchwardens and parochial church councils
disagree with these beliefs and want their churchyards to be neat and tidy. It is
easy to understand their views, but there are many churchyards where both
the clearance and leaving it to nature approach has worked beautifully. You
have only to visit All Saints at Binfield to appreciate how it is possible to
combine the two. This churchyard has its own wild flower sanctuary where
there are said to be seventy three different varieties of plant. Another churchyard, at St Mary the Virgin, Burghfield, has sixty four different species.

Certainly churchyard conservation has become much more important in
recent years – we are more aware of the natural beauty to be found in these
places and the need for it to be nurtured and protected. Wild birds, insects,
plants, wild flowers, all belong in this peaceful habitat.

Grass sometimes covers the gravestones, particularly ledger stones and
children's gravestones, which are smaller and closer to the ground. Many

times I have peeled the grass back like a mat to reveal the hidden epitaph. But, as John Betjeman believed, it must be better to use a goat like the one I saw in St Michael's churchyard, Clifton Hampden, happily munching at the grass, than a lawnmower and shears.

If the wildlife flourishes in a churchyard and the paths and graves are still accessible then the right balance has been struck. Trees and bushes are important to the overall look of the churchyard, but they also play their part in the natural way of life as well as providing symbolism – such as holly bushes and some other evergreens representing eternal life. Trees such as elms, cedars, limes, beech and horse chestnut can all be found in or around most churchyards, but yew trees seem to predominate.

During my research I discovered many instances of terrible waste of life, sometimes caused by freak weather such as when Henry West was blown off the railway station roof at Reading, or cases of drowning, like the young brothers Harold and Ernest Deverell, who lost their lives at Lower Basildon.

The poignancy of parents' anguish can be read again and again on gravestones recording the deaths of beloved children – in some cases all the children in a family, usually from some disease like typhoid, or a terrible accident. Yet still I never found the searching and recording morbid or depressing. It was more uplifting, sometimes almost joyous, as when discovering Agatha Christie's grave, after a long drive and search for the church, at Cholsey, and reflective when dwelling on the life of the person beneath the gravestone such as the wonderful Caleb Gould, buried at Remenham Hill.

I believe that reverence should be felt for our churchyards' beauty, timelessness, sense of history and the contentment contained within their boundaries. The monuments and gravestones are subject to continuous weathering and erosion. They are not only part of this country's heritage, but also a not unimportant source for local and family history. They need to be recorded and photographed, for so many are being removed and just stacked around the edges of some of the churchyards.

All Saints, Binfield

Diana Costin
1998

5

ACKNOWLEDGEMENTS

There are many people, businesses and organisations without whose help this book could not have been written. They include: Jane Alvey at Wokingham Public Library; Ted Smith, Toastmaster, House of Commons; Red Woodidge; Pangbourne Fire Brigade; Jayne Harris, New Zealand High Commission; CL Torrero of The Patent Office; the Rt Rev John Bone, Bishop of Reading; *Wokingham Times*; BBC Radio Berkshire; Barbara Young; The Rev Simon Baynes; Stanley D Snellings; Margaret Gibson; David Brazier; JFJ Bayliss; Sheila Hancock; Mrs MAL Saunders of Oxford Diocesan Advisory Committee; David Arscott; Donald Sinden; Douglas Turner; Chad Hanna, Monumental Inscriptions Coordinator, Berkshire; the Rev Ian Randall, Rector of Clewer; Tony Bennett, Swallowfield House; The Family History Society. My thanks to all of them, and to my family for their love and support.

Thomas Melrose's grave in Clewer.

BIBLIOGRAPHY

Royal Berkshire, Tom Middleton, Barracuda Books, 1975.

English Churchyard Memorials, F Burgess, Lutterworth Press, 1963.

The Old Berkshire Village Book, Berkshire Federation of WI, Countryside Books, 1985.

Records of the Parish of Wokingham, compiled Canon B Long, OUP, 1937.

Murray's Berkshire Architectural Guide, edited John Betjeman and John Piper, John Murray, 1949.

Discovering Epitaphs, Geoffrey N Wright, Shire Books, 1972.

Hidden Berkshire, Berkshire Federation of WI, Countryside Books, 1991.

Perdita – The Memoirs of Mary Robinson, edited MJ Levy, Peter Owen, 1994.

Windsor in Victorian Times, written and published by Angus MacNaughten, 1975.

Clewer – a Historic Miscellany, Denis Shaw, 1995.

Windsor Castle, Olwen Hedley, Robert Hale, 1994.

Court at Windsor, Christopher Hibbert, Longmans Green, 1962.

The Duchess of Windsor, Michael Bloch, George Weidenfeld & Nicholson, 1988.

The Times.

The Berkshire Chronicle.

ACCIDENTAL DEATHS

NO matter at what age a life is snatched away the tragedy is in the unexpectedness of the death. Lying at rest in the churchyards of Berkshire are men, women and children whose lives have been ended by accident. Their epitaphs make poignant and revealing reading. As well as such natural causes as lightning strikes, death by drowning and fatalities in storms, there are unusual accidents in far away places and bizarre incidents closer to home.

In the churchyard of St John the Baptist, Shottesbrooke, is the grave of a village blacksmith. On completion of the church in 1337 he had climbed to the top of the spire to fix the weathervane. While there, it is said, he demanded a pot of ale so that he could drink the health of the king. This loyal toast caused him to lose his balance and fall to his death.

His grave – the first in the churchyard – is on the exact spot where he landed. On his tombstone are inscribed two 'O's, the only words he uttered as he fell.

Another fatal fall from a church tower occurred in 1729. On the north side of the tower of St James's Church, Ruscombe, a small stone set into the ground marks the spot where Elizabeth Grove fell off a ladder when taking lunch to her father who

Muriel Kelsey's grave.

was carrying out repairs to the tower. Regrettably her epitaph is so weathered it is illegible.

Falls from lesser heights were responsible for the deaths, in different centuries, of Thomas Day and Muriel Kelsey. Day was a philosopher and the author of fifteen books including *Sandford and Merton*, a best-selling school story written for boys. In September 1789, on the way to visit his mother, he was thrown from the unbroken colt he was riding and fell on his head, sustaining a fatal injury. His wife died three years later of a broken heart and was buried by his side in St Mary's churchyard at Wargrave. The epitaph was destroyed in a fire but it had read:

In memory of
Thomas Day Esq.,
Who died the 28th of September, 1789
Aged 41
After having promoted by the Energy
of his Writing,
And encouraged by the Uniformity of
his Example,
The unremitted exercise of
Every public and private
Virtue.

Muriel Kelsey, an only child, apparently died when her horse fell with her. On her tombstone are the words:

In loving memory of Muriel,
Dearly beloved and only child of
JOHN AND ANNIE KELSEY,
Suddenly called home by her horse
falling with her,
On the evening of Oct:18th 1917,
aged 23 years.
She shall not return to us. We shall
go to her.

Three people froze to death in Berkshire in the terrible winter of 1881. *The Berkshire Chronicle* reported that George Hawkins, aged forty, was found with his horse still alive beside him on the morning of 26 January, a mere 150 yards from his home. At the inquest it was said that people heard cries for help at about 9pm the previous night but did not go and investigate. The cause of death was confirmed as due to exposure to the cold and the inquest jury censured those who had heard George's cries and had not helped.

George was buried at St Mark's, Cold Ash, but his gravestone is now in a closed section of the churchyard. At St Michael's, Inkpen, there is a cross cut into a brick garden wall. It marks where Thomas Bailey, a sixty-seven year old labourer, died of cold in the great snowstorm of 18 January 1881, within 100 yards of his home. He had spent the day threshing in Kintbury and had collapsed from exhaustion at about 7.30 pm. John Panting had assisted him back to Inkpen and when Thomas assured him that he was all right, John went to the pub. An hour and a half later Thomas was found nearly dead. He had only enough strength to lift one hand before he expired.

A younger victim of that snowstorm was eleven year old William Thatcher. He had been with three men delivering coal to Lambourne when snow started to fall. They lost their way on the Downs and wandered about for hours. William collapsed, and after being carried for more than two hours he died before they could all be rescued. His epitaph at St Mary's, Longcott, reads:

He has gone from our midst
tho' tis but for a while
With pleasure though mingled
with pain
We will think of his sayings and trea-
sure his smile
And look on to our meeting again.

Victims of the weather in summer were Joseph Buxey, sixty-four, and

In Memory

JOSEPH BIXEY
AGED 64 YEARS

GEORGE PALMER
AGED 32 YEARS

Who were killed by Lightning under one
of the trees at Kirby June 16th 1857.

This Stone is raised by the Parishioners.
St. Luke XIII. 4.5.

Joseph Bixby and George Palmer.

George Palmer, thirty-two. On 16 June 1857 they were both struck by lightning. Their gravestone is on the right of the lychgate under a yew hedge in St Michael's churchyard, Inkpen.

It was among the snows of the Alps that twenty-two year old Bulkley Samuel Young, who is buried in Holy Trinity churchyard, Cookham, lost his life. The accident is described in this letter sent from the Hotel de Chamonix on 24 August 1866, written by an Edwin Pettitt. 'I regret to inform you that a sad accident occurred yesterday whereby another life has been sacrificed. Sir George Young, with two brothers and a cousin, successfully reached the summit of Mont Blanc (without guides) yesterday, at 10 am, and were descending to the grand plateau when a mass of snow gave way, precipitating the younger brother down a frightful slope of snow. The brothers descended to the Grand Mulets to despatch a messenger to Chamounix for assistance, but the accident having been witnessed by a gentleman who had informed the chef de guide, a party of eleven guides and a doctor had already left for Grand Mulets. A letter was sent down this morning by Sir George, informing us of the sad loss of his brother, and this morning at 10.30 the guides with Sir George reached the fatal spot.'

When a whirlwind struck the Great Western Railway's station at Reading on 24 March 1840, it claimed the life of Henry West. He was working on a large lantern-like wooden structure on top of the waiting room which was being built next to the station house. Although it weighed four tons this 'lantern' was carried by the

Bulkley Young's gravestone.

Henry West's impressive oak grave marker at Reading.

whirlwind right over the station house, where it hit a chimney before crashing to the ground. Henry's body was found 200 yards away among the debris.

A number of other people were injured but Henry was the only fatality. When he was buried in St Laurence's churchyard his workmates put up a handsome wooden grave marker 'in affectionate respect to his memory'. It has been renewed three times over the years – by his brother George in 1862, by his niece FG Rixon in 1924 and in 1971 by 'Reading Corporation'.

Fate appears to have taken a hand in the accidental demise of Richard, Earl of Barrymore. At the age of twenty-three, having been married for only eight months, he was on horseback military escort duty in Dover, accompanying French prison-ers of war, when he dropped his rifle which was loaded and primed. It exploded and he was shot in the head and killed. He was not mourned in Wargrave where, some years previously, he had built a theatre. It is said that upon his death the theatre was ripped to pieces by local business-men eager to recover some of the money owed to them. The family, fearing that the corpse would be abused or spirited away, had it interred on 17 March 1793 in a unmarked grave in the chancel of St Mary's Church.

Sixteen year old William White, who worked for a Mr Cokes of Hampstead Marshall, and lies in the churchyard of St John the Divine, Stockcross, was a more tragic victim of an accidental gunshot. He was sweeping up the back kitchen when Mr Cokes' nephew, a young boy

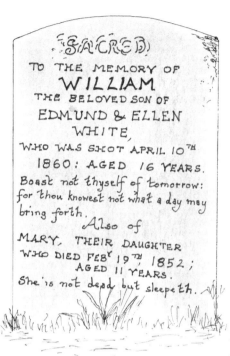

SACRED

TO THE MEMORY OF

WILLIAM

THE BELOVED SON OF

EDMUND & ELLEN
WHITE,
WHO WAS SHOT APRIL 10ᵀᴴ
1860: AGED 16 YEARS.
Boast not thyself of tomorrow:
for thou knowest not what a day may
bring forth.
Also of
MARY, THEIR DAUGHTER
WHO DIED FEBʳ 19ᵀᴴ 1852;
AGED 11 YEARS.
She is not dead but sleepeth.

*The headstone of shot
teenager William White.*

called Charles Burton, picked up a gun and not thinking it was loaded, cocked it to let the cap off to frighten a dog. At that moment William stooped to pick up a broom and was shot in the head. He died at about 3am the next morning, 10 April 1860.

In less safety conscious and socially aware days tragedies at work accounted for many accidental deaths. The gravestones of Berkshire tell their sad stories.

There is Charles Dearmarsh, employed by H Hippesley, who fell from a tree whilst lopping it and was killed on the spot, in February, 1869. The inquest verdict was accidental death. He left a widow and one child whom, Mr Hippesley said, were to be well provided for. Perhaps this was an early case of compensation.

John Hopwood, who is buried in St Mary's churchyard, Shinfield, was sitting on a water barrel on the farm where he worked when a horse shied and kicked out. John fell off and the wheel of the cart that the horse was pulling passed over his stomach. He was taken to hospital but died on 20 August 1869 from his injuries.

The 'melancholy fatal accident' which brought George Franklin to his grave in St Bartholomew's churchyard, Arborfield, is described in *The Berkshire Chronicle* in 1884. He was thrown from his cart and killed while on his rounds for the butcher in Broad Street, Reading, for whom he worked. 'No one saw the accident, but he was found lying in the road with the horse still attached to the cart lying on top of him,' says the report.

At St Michael's Church, Enbourne, is a stone erected by subscription to the memory of Frederick Gibbs, who was killed at the Grammar School on October 3, 1884, aged twenty-one. He was one of the contractors building the new school in Newbury. A shaft was being sunk on the site to obtain gravel and sand, and the men had excavated to a depth of about twelve feet through a solid bed of gravel, when the top portion of the shaft suddenly shelled out with sufficient force to break the chief timber work, letting the whole structure down with the mass of gravel behind it. Two men were buried beneath the debris. One was rescued after twenty minutes with his legs broken, and fifty-five minutes later Frederick Gibbs was brought out dead.

Ernest Mumford was a member of the Pangbourne Voluntary Fire Brigade. He lived opposite the Fire Station and on June 16, 1913, was dashing out to answer a call to a farm fire, when he was knocked down by a car. His injuries appeared slight, but a week later he developed lockjaw and died in the Royal Berkshire Hospital. He is buried in the churchyard of St James

Tragic racer Vivian Lewis's grave.

the Less, Pangbourne, with a splendid stone fireman's helmet and axe on the top of the tombstone. The epitaph reads:

In loving memory of
Ernest James Mumford
who died on the 16th June 1931
from injuries received when
reporting for duty
aged 30 years
For many years second engineer
in Pangbourne and District
Fire Brigade.

Twyford Station was the scene of a fatal accident on September 11, 1865. Hannah Smith, aged sixty-three, was travelling by train with her son from Reading to Henley. Neither of them realised that they had to change trains at Twyford. When the son heard from a fellow passenger that they should do so, he opened the door of the carriage as the train was about to move

The splendid fireman's helmet and axe on Ernest Mumford's gravestone

12

off and jumped out. He fell on the platform and consequently was unable to assist his mother who was following him out of the – by then – slowly moving train. Her clothes became entangled in the handle of the carriage and she was thrown under the train behind the carriage in which she had been riding. She died about fifteen minutes after her removal to a nearby hotel. Her gravestone is at the back of St Mary's Church, Twyford.

An unusual and more recent transport-related accidental death was that of forty year old Vivian Lewis of Cookham Dean, who was killed in

An impressive memorial to two drowned sons.

her Trojeiro Jaguar when it spun off Brighton Promenade at 100mph on September 14, 1963. Her husband, David Lewis, a commercial artist, together with crowds of holidaymakers who were watching the Brighton Speed Trials, saw her car hit the kerb, somersault and crash into a childrens playground before bursting into flames. Vivian's grave is in All Saint's churchyard, Bisham.

From the evidence of epitaphs, drowning was once the most common cause of accidental death in Berkshire. Edward and Priscilla Deverell had moved to Church Farm at Basildon, a village between Pangbourne and Goring in 1885. They had two sons, Harold and Ernest, who could not swim, but loved to bathe in a side stream of the Thames near their home. The backwater was also used as a sheep dip and in part of it an eight feet deep trench had been dug. On June 26, 1886, Ernest was the first to enter the water. He fell into the trench and was immediately out of his depth and in difficulties. Harold tried to save him, but both boys, aged fifteen and sixteen, were drowned. Their distraught parents erected this monument in the churchyard of St Bartholomew, Lower Basildon, and very shortly afterwards left the area. The epitaph includes the words: '*They were lovely and pleasant in their lives, and in their death they were not divided.*'

Inside St Catherine's Church, Bear

Maude Willcocks' grave.

Wood, is a monument to John Balson Walter, son of the John Walter whose grandfather founded *The Times*. He was drowned at the age of twenty-six, attempting to rescue his brother and cousin from a frozen lake. The monument, dated 1870, shows a guardian angel with a relief below of a frozen lake.

Death by drowning claimed all ages. How did it come about that the child of nine, who is buried in St Mary the Virgin churchyard, Purley, was accidentally drowned in July, 1856? And in what circumstances was Ezekiel James Saunders, aged twelve, drowned while bathing in the Thames on June 7, 1858? His tomb-stone is in Clewer churchyard.

More than children, however, the gravestones tell of drowning accidents involving young men and women in their twenties and thirties – perhaps casting off adult responsibilities and frolicking in the Thames with disastrous results.

Frank Broaderick accidentally drowned at Cookham on September 11, 1891, aged twenty-five. He was under-coachman at a house in the village, and a strong swimmer. He said he was going to swim near the weir and left his clothes tied up in a bundle on the bank. He was found naked in the water near Cookham and, by the marks on his face, it was assumed he had struck something underneath the water.

Maude Willcock's epitaph – in a beautiful spot in All Saint's churchyard, Bisham, close to the river that runs along beside the gravestones – tells its own story.

In Loving Memory of
Maude, the dear Wife of
Charles J. Willcock, of
16 Warwick Square, S.W.
Born 23rd. July 1867
married 15th August 1890
accidentally drowned near
this spot on 3rd June 1902.
Until the day break and the
shadows flee away
Peace at last.

Another young girl in her twenties was Helen Frances Warner, who went swimming with her two sisters at

A Titanic victim's grave.

Temple Weir, Bisham on August 14, 1888. Helen, who was twenty-four, and the wife of William Warner, was not a very good swimmer and got into difficulties. She was dragged to the shore where efforts were made to revive her both before and when the doctor arrived, but to no avail.

An epitaph at St Peter's church, Woolhampton, remembers twenty-two year old Enoch Honey, who was found drowned at Aldermaston Lock on 12 January, 1876.

And snowy was the night
Sad his lot to lose his life
God's will be done.

It was not the Thames, but the Atlantic Ocean that claimed the life of teenager Owen George Allum whose grave is in St Andrew's Churchyard, Clewer. Owen was a Windsor telegraph boy. His parents were separated and, because of his mothers' ill health, he was sent to join his father in New York. The ship he sailed on was the *Titanic* and, together with so many others, he lost his life on April 14, 1912. His body was taken to New York, but it was decided that as his sister was already buried in Clewer churchyard, Owen should be brought home for burial. His tombstone reads:

Here Rests in Christ
OWEN GEORGE ALUM
Shipwrecked on the Titanic
and drowned at sea, April 14th 1912
Aged 17 Years
Nearer My God To Thee.

In July 1989 the gravestone was vandalised. When Denis Cochrane, a master at the Cardinal Vaughan Memorial School, Kensington, and a collector of Titanic memorabilia, heard it had been damaged, he and five pupils went to Clewer and worked for a day repairing the stone and renewing the lettering with black enamel.

Other epitaphs recording accidental deaths

Sacred
To the Memory of
CHARLOTTE,
Daughter of William
and Elizabeth Smith
who died of Smallpox
November 27th 1849
Aged 31 years

St Mary's, Shinfield

Here Lyeth
The Body Of
FANNY GOSLING
Who was Killed by an
Accident on the Railway in a most
awful
and sudden manner.
St Michael, Clifton Hampden

In the midst of life we are in death
Here rests in hope
Robert James Piggott
who in the hour of health and
amusement
was called away by most sudden
death
March lst 1850
Aged 48 years
Watch therefore for ye know not
whathour your Lord doth come.
St Mary, Reading

Too many trains
Not enough stations.
St Bartholomew, Arborfield

Near to the body
of Elizabeth RUSS
who died May 30,1859
Aged 81
Lies the body of her husband
and lieth the remains of JOSEPH
who was accidentally killed by the
fall of a
tree October l5th 1817, aged 47.
Hampstead Marshall Parish Church

In Memory of
WILLIAM HENRY PULLEN,

Who Died 5th of June 1813,
Aged 27 Years.
Scarce does the Sun each
morning rise
And close its evening Ray
Without some human sacrifice
Some tragic scene display.
A shocking accident occurred
Alas with Grief I tell
The youth who now lies here interred
To Death a victim fell.
Well could he drive the coursers fleet
Which oft he drove before
Where turning round a narrow Street
He fell to rise no more.
No one commanded more respect,
Obliging, kind and fair,
None charged him with the
least neglect
Nor drove with greater care.
He little thought when he arose
The fatal fifth of June
That morn his life's career
would close
And terminate so soon.
Though snatched from Earth we hope
and trust
He's called to Joy's abode
Virtues like his so pure and just
Ensure celestial Love. L.N.
Holy Trinity, Cookham

ANIMALS

ONE of the best kept secrets in the county is an animal graveyard hidden away in the depths of Swallowfield Park. The history of the park and the house is as interesting as the graveyard itself.

Swallowfield House dates back to the Norman Conquest. For ten years – 1727 to 1737 – it was owned by Thomas Pitt, whose second son, William, became Prime Minister at the age of twenty-five. Thomas inherited Swallowfields from his father, Diamond Pitt, so called because he is said to have brought home from India, hidden in the heel of his son's shoe, a 400 carat diamond, part of which became a jewel in Napoloen's sword hilt.

Sir Henry Russell, the retired Chief Justice of Bengal, bought Swallowfield in 1820 and made many alterations. The house and park passed through several generations of the Russell family – Sir Henry's descendents being soldiers or men of action, scholars and the friends of writers and members of parliament.

In 1965 the property was sold to the Country Houses Association, a charity whose main objective is to save, for the benefit of the nation, buildings of historic interest and architectural importance, together with their gardens and grounds.

The association's founder, Rear-Admiral Bernard Wilberforce Greathed, had the unusual idea of not only saving important yet decaying country houses, but of providing accommodation for members of the armed forces who were returning to the United Kingdom.

Swallowfield Park House is now home to 'active retired' people from

The animal graves at Swallowfield Park.

all walks of life. Residents have their own private apartments. Their fees help to maintain the house.

The park, open to the public, is approached from the quadrangle through an avenue of clipped yews said to be some 300 years old. At the end of this avenue is the Talman Gate which leads to a walled garden built by Diamond Pitt in 1722, and repaired in 1989 by Anneka Rice and the team from the BBC Television show *Challenge Anneka*.

Through an apple orchard on the right hand side is a door leading to a shady grass walk, and there in a secluded spot overlooking fields, lie all the animals buried in Swallowfield Park for the last 100 years.

Among the three rows of small headstones is one to the well travelled companion of an army colonel:

CHAD BRETT
A MUCH LOVED LABRADOR
BORN NIGERIA 1965
TRAVELLED IN W. INDIES
S ARABIA AND FINLAND.
DIED 11.8.1977.

In the next row lie two dogs who died whilst fighting each other.

GREENIE AND SYLVINA
WHO BOTH MET WITH THE
SAME CRUEL FATE
MAY THOUTH REMOTE FROM
PAIN AND STRIFE
ENJOY ANOTHER HAPPY LIFE
IN ONE ELYSIAN FIELD OF LIGHT
WHERE DOGS ARE

NOT ALLOWED TO FIGHT
1918.

If Greenie and Sylvina were involved in undercover dog fighting then their grave must be one of the very few to be found in Berkshire. Until it was condemned in 1832, annual bull baiting was a big day in most towns' calenders. Spectators would crowd round the market place in their hundreds to watch as the bull with a rope round his horns and a chain fifteen feet long would be led into the middle of the crowd by a dozen or so strong men. The chain would be fastened to a strong staple in a post level with the ground. On the command 'Set On!' a dog would be released to tear towards the bull through hoops held at regular intervals in front of the bull. Many times the bull's horns would either injure the dog so badly he died almost immediately, or would toss him into the air so that he crashed to the ground and was killed. One bull-baiting reported at Wokingham in 1815 said that the dog was tossed so high he fell onto the roof of the Town Hall and was impaled on some spikes.

Records do not exist of where the bodies of these dogs were buried – or if, indeed, they were buried.

Next to the grave for the two dogs stands a gravestone for another pair:

HERE LIE
DEAR MAX AND LITTLE SHEILA
PLAYMATES IN LIFE,
BY DEATH THEY WERE NOT

LONG DIVIDED.
OCTOBER 1922
TO HAPPY HUNTING GROUNDS
WE HOPE THEY ARE FLED
BUT, OH THEIR GRASSY MOUNDS
WE'RE LEFT OUR TEARS TO SHED.

**Other little gravestones in
Swallowfields Park read:**

HERE LIES
DEAR GENTLE MORO
LOVED IN LIFE AND
MOURNED IN DEATH
DIED 8TH NOV 1915

RIP WAS HIS NAME
HIS EPITAPH THE SAME
DIED 1904
AGED 15

ALAS! POOR TRILBY
DIED 1903

VITA
DIED 1908

QUEST
BORN JAN 16TH 1936
DIED JAN 1ST 1938

Right at the front, in the middle of these special gravestones, is the most famous – for Bumble. This dog belonged to Charles Dickens who named his animal after the character in *Oliver Twist*. The epitaph includes these words:

THEY KNOW NOT OF THAT

Bumble's grave.

EMINENCE WHICH MARKS HIM
TO MY REASONING SENSE;
THEY KNOW BUT THINK HE IS
A MAN, AND STILL TO THEM IS
KIND AND GLADS THEM ALL HE CAN.

When Dickens died in 1870 Bumble was given to Sir Charles Russell and he remained at Swallowfield Park for many years, prized and loved by all.

Behind Bumble's grave is that of Grannie, 'the mother of all the cats', who died in 1908.

Another dog that travelled far and wide during his life was Towser. His headstone recalls the adventures of the 'dear and faithful companion' who travelled with the 17th Lancers to Copenhagen, Jeypore, Agra, Gwalor, Bombay, Malta, Shorncliffe, Hounslow, Preston, Birmingham, York and Ballinkolig. Towser was born in St Petersburg in 1888 and died at Swallowfield Park in 1901.

What a dog this must have been and what a contrast for him to have lived in places like Jeypore or St Petersberg and then Birmingham or Hounslow.

Close by is an epitaph to:

DEAR CHRYS
DIED 3RD NOV: 1916
I GRIEVED FOR THEE, AND
WISHED THY END WERE PAST
AND WILLINGLY HAVE LAID
THEE HERE AT LAST,
FOR THOU HADST LIVED TILL
EVERYTHING THAT CHEERS
IN THEE HAD YIELDED TO THE
WEIGHT OF YEARS
EXTREME OLD AGE HAD WASTED THEE
AWAY AND LEFT THEE
BUT A GLIMMERING OF THE DAY
DEATH CAME
AND I WAS GLAD
YET TEARS WERE SHED
FOR MAUD WEPT THOU WERE DEAD.

No one at Swallowfield knows who Maud may have been; possibly she was the owner of this brave old animal.

There is a barely legible headstone to Royal, a 'humble and gentle' dog, another remembering Tray, a 'waif and stray' who died in 1915, and a more modern grave where Sophie, a chihuahua who died in 1995, is buried.

One of the strangest gravestones says:

RUFFIE, BLACKIE
AND CINDY
WHOSE FATES WERE

WRAPT IN MYSTERY
1915-16

Did they all go missing and were never seen again or did something worse happen to them? No amount of research unearthed the story behind this epitaph.

There is one animal gravestone at Swallowfield Park that is, for some reason, well away from the others. The inscription says:

SWALLOWFIELD
TANDY
9TH JUNE 1935
2ND OCT 1948.

The graves of 'Dear Chrys' and, behind, of Grannie, 'the mother of all the cats'.

Swallowfield Park is open to the public during the summer months for two afternoons a week.

Lady Mabel Cholmondeley, who lived at Leigh House, Datchet, in the early years of the twentieth century, owned at least thirty cats. When each one died she buried it in a coffin and erected a gravestone to its memory. When she died in 1928, her Will stated that if Leigh House were sold and redeveloped, her cats' burial places should be left undisturbed.

In 1930 Leigh House was demolished and an estate of houses built in its place. Lady Cholmondeley's

20

The island of shrubs at Leigh Park, all that remains of the cats' cemetery that Lady Mabel Cholmondeley asked should remain undisturbed.

wishes were honoured and an island of shrubs containing her cats' cemetery was left in the middle of the road. No sign of the gravestones remain, but the little island is a living monument to the cats she loved so much.

In the garden of Adelaide Cottage, Frogmore, which had once belonged to Queen Charlotte, Queen Victoria buried Dash, the companion of her girlhood, whose epitaph she herself is said to have composed:

Here lies DASH
The favourite Spaniel of Her Majesty
Queen Victoria

By whose command this memorial
was erected.
He died on the 20th December 1840,
In his ninth year.
His attachment was without
selfishness,
His playfulness without malice,
His fidelity without deceit.
Reader,
If you would live beloved and die
regretted,
Profit by the example of
DASH.

ARMED SERVICES

THE churchyards of Berkshire, like those in any other county, are full of the graves of men and women who have fought for their country through the centuries.

They are members of an elite force that holds steadfastly to virtues and values which have been constantly eroded in life outside the services. When Field Marshall Montgomery retired he said that among the impressions he would take with him was 'the picture of the British soldier – staunch, tenacious in adversity, kind and gentle in victory, the man to whom the nation has again and again in the hour of peril owed its safety and its honour'.

It is certain that those sentiments were meant as much for the sailor as for the soldier, or the pilot, or the thousands of individuals serving in the many other services that have helped to keep the peace.

At St John the Baptist Church, Padworth, you will see a stone tablet on the east wall of the porch, placed there in 1894. It commemorates the discovery of a mixed collection of human remains, lying very near the surface, which were believed to be those of three hundred men who lost their lives in 1643. They were Parliamentary troops who were retiring after the Battle of Newbury, making their way towards London, when they were surprised by a company of Prince Ruperts' horsemen and killed in the skirmish. The epitaph reads:

To the Nameless Dead
who lie near
Supposed to be soldiers
who fell in an encounter
in Aldermaston Lane
Between the forces of
King Charles the
First and
the Parliament
21st September 1643

When soldiers died in the eighteenth and nineteenth century, they were usually buried where they fell, or nearby, and in their own churchyards at home gravestones or wall plaques were erected to their memory.

Lieutenant Dexter who died in the eighteenth century, was buried in India, but his sword was returned to his wife Mary, who lived at Kintbury in Berkshire. Mary was the daughter of the Reverend Fowle who had connections with the writer Jane Austen. Thomas C Fowle was engaged to Cassandra, Jane Austen's sister, but he died of yellow fever in the West Indies before they could be married. However, the Austen sisters kept up their friendship with the Fowle family and often went to stay with them in Kintbury. When Mary Dexter died, her husband's sword was placed in her coffin. Ever since there has been a legend that if you walk through the churchyard of St Mary's, Kintbury, you may hear Lieutenant Dexter's sword rattling.

In 1786, John Hoult, who was in the Royal Regiment Horse Guards under Major Staveley, died aged thirty four. It is not clear from his epitaph whether he died in battle or from one of the many diseases that so often claimed soldiers' lives when they lived in such terrible conditions. His gravestone is in St Mary the Virgin's churchyard, Speen, and is adorned with the swords and plumes associated with battle. It reads:

JOHN HOULT
Late of Major
STAVELEY's
Troop. Royal Regiment
Horfe Guards
Departed
this Life 22nd March
1786. Aged 34 Years
Here fleeps
within this filent Grave
A loyal Soldier, Juft and Brave
After a fhort and fudden shock
Content he did his Live give up.
Till the laft trumpets awful found
He is here in fettled
quarters bound

Two young men who also died in their thirties were in the Royal Horse Guards and both lost their lives in 1811. George Smith died on June 5, aged thirty one, and was buried in St Andrew's Church, Clewer. Inscribed

on his tombstone are the words:
My sledge and hammer lies declined
My bellows, too, have
lost their wind
My fires extinct, my Forge decayed
My vice is in the dust now laid.
My coat is spent, my iron gone
My nails are drove, my work is done

This is almost overwhelming in its eloquence and could easily have been the kind of epitaph seen on a much older soldier's gravestone.

In contrast David George's epitaph is straight to the point. He also died in 1811, on December 20, after serving thirteen years in the Royal Horse Guards. He was thirty two.

My warning short,
my time is come.
Christ called me
hence my
Glass is run.

The Battle of Waterloo looms large in British history and there are a number of churchyards in Berkshire which bear testimony to some of its soldiers.

In the churchyard of St Michael, Clifton Hampden, is the now hidden grave of William Dykes. It is recorded that either from excessive zeal or carelessness, he fired the first shots of the Battle of Waterloo before being given an order to do so. He was sent home in disgrace, but later pardoned by the Duke of Wellington.

John Siddall is remembered as the last surviving member of all ranks in

John Siddall's impressive monument.

the Household Brigade of Cavalry who fought that famous Battle. He was a veterinary surgeon in the Royal Regiment of Horse Guards and must have had to deal with some atrocious wounds to the poor animals who carried their brave masters into war. The suffering and hardship endured in Europe during those campaigns were recorded by many in their journals and diaries. Again and again men wrote of having to live as best they could off the country because rations were not forthcoming, whilst the cavalry horses starved for want of forage. It was said that Wellington lost four of his cavalry regiments as they were so depleted in men and horse-flesh that they had to be dismounted and sent home.

John Siddall survived the horrors of war and died on October 2, 1856, aged sixty nine. His monument is impressive and severe.

Quarter-Master Edward Adams also served in the Royal Regiment of Horse Guards but he died in the forty second year of his service whilst attending church parade in October, 1819. At his inquest the verdict recorded that his death was 'A Visitation of God'. His funeral was a grand affair and his horse, as shown in the carving on his tomb, followed the coffin with its rider's boots reversed in the stirrups.

The memorial is grand and situated close to the front porch of St. Andrew's Parish Church, Clewer.

The British public was horrified to learn of the administrative incompetence and the casualty toll in the

Edward Adams' tombstone

Crimean War in 1854. In the seven months from October of that year until the following April, thirty five per cent of the total strength of the expeditionary force died, many not from enemy action, but from sickness, malnutrition and exposure. Although this was often the case in previous battles the Crimea was unique in that it was reported back to England by a war correspondent who accompanied the army and reported all that he saw.

One immediate result was the institution of awards for acts of gallantry and distinguished conduct in the field. In August 1855 Britain's supreme award for bravery, the Victoria Cross, was instituted and was open to all ranks.

Robert Lindsay, who later became Lord Wantage, was the first man to receive the Victoria Cross. He was awarded it on June 27, 1857 from the Queen's own hands. His name had appeared earlier that year in an edition of the *London Gazette* stating that when the formation of the line was disordered at the Alma on September 20, 1854, Captain Robert James Lindsay, Brevet-Major, First Battalion Scots Fusilier Guards, stood firm with the Colours and, by his example and energy, restored order.

Later, at Inkerman (November 5), Lindsay, with a few men, charged a party of Russians, driving them back, and running one through the body himself.

Lindsay resigned from the army and became a Conservative Member of Parliament. He socialised with the Royal Family, married a rich heiress and became one of Englands' most successful farmers. He modernised British agriculture and converting the farming communities on his estates into model villages.

On July 28, 1885 the Queen conferred on him a peerage. He chose for his title the old Saxon town of Wantage, said to be the birthplace of King Alfred, and on that day he took his seat in the House of Lords as Baron Wantage of Lockinge.

Lord Wantage died on June 10, 1901 and is buried in Holy Trinity churchyard, Ardington. His marble pillar cross which is supposed to be a replica of the fifteenth century cross of San Zenobio in the Piazza del Duomo at Florence, was erected by his wife.

Also lying in the churchyard at Ardington is a nephew of Lord Wantage – Robert Hamilton Lindsay, third son of the twenty sixth Earl of Crawford. Robert Lindsay was a non-resident, but being a nephew of Lord Wantage he had been a regular visitor to the big house at Lockinge and had expressed many times that he wished to be buried in a country churchyard like Ardington.

He died, aged thirty seven, while

His family watch over the effigy of Robert Hamilton Lindsay.

stationed at York with his regiment in 1911 and in this hillside churchyard lies the plinth with a recumbent effigy, in the uniform of the guards, just as he would have wished. His head is supported by his wife in the figure of an angel and at his feet kneel his three children.

To find Louise Parson's grave it is necessary to bypass St Mary's churchyard, Shinfield, and instead head for the extra churchyard given to the church in 1902 by the Cobham family of Shinfield. They donated half an acre of ground to form an additional cemetery, which is about a hundred yards along Church Lane and down a footpath.

By 1920 this area had rapidly filled up and it was decided that in future only Shinfield parishioners would be buried there. This churchyard is now full. It is a strange place because of the number of unmarked graves which can only be located by noting their position against marked gravestones. No other churchyard seen in Berkshire held so many lumpy, awkwardly covered graves that lie around this area like strange creatures with nowhere else to go. Sheep are let in to graze the churchyard and no doubt have trouble scaling these strange burial mounds to nibble the grass.

Louise Parsons was a nursing sister who served with the army in the Egyptian Campaign of 1882. She was decorated with the Khedive (a medal with Queen Victoria on one side, the Sphinx on the reverse) for her brave and devoted nursing during the war. She also received the Royal Red Cross Award from Queen Victoria for her nursing in the Boer and Spanish-American Wars. All through these wars the Red Cross and the Army Medical Department worked together in harmony to alleviate the suffering of the sick and wounded soldiers and other victims of war. Louise must have been a remarkable woman.

Her grave is in the churchyard of St Mary, at Shinfield.

IN LOVING MEMORY OF
SISTER EMMA, WHO DIED 1912
ALSO OF
LOUISA PARSONS
SISTER OF THE ABOVE
NURSING SISTER OF THE BRITISH ARMY
FOUNDER OF UNIVERSITY OF
MARYLAND TRAINING SCHOOL U.S.A.,
NOBLE AND DEVOTED NURSE OF THE
EGYPTIAN CAMPAIGN, BOER AND
SPANISH-AMERICAN WARS
DECORATED BY THE KHEDIVE, AND WITH
THE ROYAL RED CROSS
BY QUEEN VICTORIA
DIED NOVEMBER 2ND 1916
AGED 58 YEARS.

In St John the Baptist churchyard, Crowthorne, is a simple headstone to the memory of a soldier whose epitaph speaks for itself:

In Memory of
LT. COLONEL SERVAIS
BELGIAN OFFICER
WHO DIED FAR FROM HIS FATHERLAND
AMONGST KIND HEARTED
ENGLISH PEOPLE
MAY 1ST 1919. AGED 76 YEARS.

Sir Charles Brownlow, born in 1831, entered the Army rather late for those times, aged twenty six. But he rose rapidly in the ranks, achieving the post of field marshall after serving in the Punjab wars and various Indian campaigns. For his services in the Ambeyla Campaign he received the Order of the Companion of the Bath, followed by a knighthood in 1877. After his retirement from the army he was appointed ADC to Queen Victoria.

Sir Charles was fifty nine when he married Georgina, eldest daughter of W C King of Warfield Hall. In 1912, when his wife died, he decided to give away his money in gifts to the parish. He repaired the church tower in her memory and then planned a new parish hall. This was completed after his death and called the Brownlow Hall as his memorial. He died in 1916 and was buried in the churchyard of St Michael the Archangel, Warfield.

In the churchyard of St Michael and Mary Magdalene, Easthampstead, is the tombstone of a man who was not only a great soldier but an intrepid explorer as well.

27

At the age of twenty six Frederick George Jackson made his first voyage with a whaling expedition in Arctic water. He then completed a 3,000 mile journey across the Siberian tundra, writing about his experiences in a book called *The Frozen Land.*

As a result of this success he was appointed commander of the Jackson-Harmsworth Expedition. For this trip Frederick Jackson designed all kinds of polar equipment, from weather-proof cooking stoves to special tents and sleeping bags. During the trip they were said to have rescued the Norwegian Explorer Fridtjof Nansen, who had been missing for two years. Nansen claimed later that he would have been able to get home unaided!

Jackson wrote a popular second travel story called *A Thousand Days in the Arctic.* He was given the Royal Humane Society's medal in 1885, the Danish Royal Order of St Olaf in 1898 and the gold medal of the Societé Géographique the following year.

He then decided to become a soldier and joined the East Surrey Regiment to fight the Boers.

He died aged seventy eight on March 13, 1938, and was given a memorial service in St Paul's Cathedral, before being laid to rest in Easthampstead Churchyard. His epitaph includes these words:

I never see a map but I'm away
On all the journeys that
I long to do
Up all the rivers that are painted
blue
And all the ranges that are painted
grey
And into these pale spaces where
they say – UNKNOWN.

Another officer who must have had little time in his short life for much else besides soldiering was Major A J Moorhouse, who was born on September 11, 1891, and who served with the 12th Manchester Regiment. He died on November 28, 1918 and was buried at St Peter's, Cranbourne. His very impressive memorial is situated close to a rambling hedge that is full of blossom and birdsong in the spring.

Berkshire seems to have its share of great generals, and certainly General Sir Miles Dempsey, who died in 1969, at the age of seventy two, was an accomplished soldier. Although he was mentioned in despatches and awarded the Military Cross, he was virtually unknown to the general public.

He was born on December 15, 1896. At Shrewsbury he captained the first cricket eleven for three years and after a course at Sandhurst was commissioned in The Royal Berks Regiment. In the First World War he served from 1916 to 1918 on the Western front where he commanded a company when only nineteen years of age.

Miles Dempsey was gassed in 1918, but after a few months in hospital he served in the Mesopotamia (Iraq) Campaign of 1919-1920. He was a keen student of military history and visited battlefields on the Continent between the wars, making carefully indexed maps.

In 1939 he was Commanding Officer with the First Berkshire when they landed in France. Later, he took command of the Thirteenth Infantry Brigade which played an outstanding part in the British counter attack at

General Sir Miles Dempsey's grave at Yattendon.

Arras in May 1940, thus gaining valuable time for the withdrawl from Dunkirk.

Dempsey retired at the age of fifty in 1946, and he died on June 6, 1969. His grave is in the churchyard of St Peter and Paul at Yattendon.

Another general who received numerous decorations and awards throughout his military career was Brigadier General Sir Herbert William Wilberforce.

Educated at Eton and Sandhurst, he entered the Army in 1886, became a captain in 1896 and was ADC to the Governor-General of Canada between 1895 and 1898. In 1900 he was promoted to major and was employed by the South African Constabulary for three years.

His grave is in the churchyard of St Mary the Virgin at Hurley. The inscription reads:

Major A J Moorhouse's memorial.

29

Brigadier General Sir Herbert Wilberforce's grave.

In Memory of
BRIGADIER GENERAL
SIR HERBERT WILLIAM WILBERFORCE
K.B.E., C.B., C.M.G.,
KNIGHT OF GRACE, ST. JOHN OF
JERUSALEM
CROIX DE COMMANDEUR
LEGION D'HONNEUR
LATE THE QUEENS BAYS

Another senior army officer, Major General Sir Edward Spears, is buried with his first wife, Mary Borden, in the churchyard at St Michael the Archangel, Warfield.

Sir Edward died on January 27, 1974, aged eighty seven. Known as Louis to his close friends, he was a talented soldier, politician, author and businessman.

In 1914, as a lieutenant of the Eleventh Hussars, he was appointed liaison officer between Sir John French, the British Commander-in-Chief, and General Lanrezac commanding the French on his right.

For the remainder of the First World War he occupied many liaison posts and achieved the rank of Brigadier-General. He was wounded four times, was awarded the Military Cross, the CBE and the CB, became a Commander of the French Legion of Honour and received the Croix de Guerre with three palms.

Sir Edward retired from the service in 1920 and went into Parliament, first as a National Liberal and then as a Conservative. In May 1940 he was sent to France by Winston Churchill to act as his representative to the French prime minister. It was Spears who selected de Gaulle as the most likely French officer to be able to reform French units overseas, and a long liaison began with the French general, ending acrimoniously when de Gaulle developed policies of his own, at variance with those of Britain.

Sir Edward received a baronetcy in 1953, returned to his business pursuits and became a leading figure in the foundation of the Institute of Directors. He wrote several volumes about his war experiences and a book of recollections of his childhood.

In 1918 he had married the novel-

The graves of Major General Sir Edward Spears, his wife, the author Mary Borden, and their only son Michael.

ist Mary Borden who was then at the beginning of her writing career (and at the same time he changed the spelling of his name from Spiers to Spears). Mary had directed a mobile hospital at the front in the First World War and received medals from both France and England, including the Croix de Guerre and Legion of Honour.

Mary, born in Chicago, had divorced her first husband in 1908. After her marriage to Spears she wrote some twenty books. She died in December, 1968.

Sir Edward married again and died one year before his second wife, Nancy, in 1974.

Naval officers are also to be found in many churchyards in Berkshire. One British sailor who became famous for introducing a new system

of signalling at sea which was used at the Battle of Trafalgar was Sir Home Riggs Popham, who is buried at St Michael's in Sunninghill.

He was born in 1762 at Tetuan (in Morocco), entered the Navy in 1778 and commanded the fleet convoying the Army which retook Cape Town in 1806. In 1807 he was court-martialled and reprimanded for undertaking an expedition, which miscarried, against Brazil. He served in the Copenhagen foray of 1808 and was knighted in 1815 – quite a remarkable feat for a man who been court-martialled. Popham led a fascinating life, travelling all over the world. He died on September 10, 1820.

Dr William Gordon-Stables was a surgeon in the Royal Navy for nine years, until he was invalided out on half-pay. He then became a profes-

31

sional author and, like so many of his armed services counterparts, wrote about his experiences in the war. Many of his books and articles were adventure stories based on his life as a commissioned assistant surgeon for the Navy. He was particularly interested in the suppression of the slave trade off Mozambique.

The doctor was born in Banffshire on May 21, 1840, died at Twyford in May, 1910 and is buried in the churchyard of St James, Ruscombe.

Dr William Gordon-Stables.

Other epitaphs to members of the armed forces

Sergeant Samuel Perkins, R.E.
Husband of Emily Perkins
who
departed this life
Nov 5 1891. Aged 56 years
Had he asked

us well we know
We should cry O spare this Blow
Yes with
streaming tears shall pray
Lord we love him, let him stay.
St John The Baptist, Crowthorne

In Memory of
A. T. THORNBY TUNBRIDGE
2ND LIEUT. 6TH ROYAL
BERKS REGT. WHO FELL
IN ACTION OCT. 12TH 1917
AGED 27 YEARS
HIS COMMANDING OFFICER SAID THAT
THE WAY IN WHICH HE HE LED HIS PLATOON
DURING THE ADVANCE WAS MAGNIFICENT
AND THAT HIS UNDAUNTED COURAGE
WAS AN EXAMPLE TO ALL. HE FOUGHT
CONTINUALLY FOR THREE YEARS FROM
THE FIRST TO THE THIRD BATTLE OF
YPRES.
St Nicholas, Remenham Hill

GEORGE FULBROOK
66TH REGT. DIED AT
KHELAT-I-GHIZAL
SOUTH AFGHANISATAN
IN THE FAITHFUL
DISCHARGE OF HIS
DUTY, JUNE 26, 1880
AGED 22.
St Mary, Shinfield

CENTENARIANS

L ONGEVITY on gravestones is not easy to find in Berkshire, but careful searching can bring about a few very interesting discoveries.

Nowadays men and women who reach the age of 100 have parties to celebrate, surrounded by their families and friends.They also receive telegrams from the Queen.

But a century or more ago even to reach the age of fifty or sixty was an accomplishment, let alone the milestone age of 100.

Men who worked long hours in fields and workshops, and women who had borne half a dozen children in poor physical and medical conditions, having seen perhaps half of them die in infancy, were apt to grow old early. The number of elderly and aged was comparatively small compared to today's elderly population.

Also the way society cared for them was very different. If they had no living relatives then it fell to the community to take care of them. This was accomplished very often by private charity which provided for the bereaved and the poor. This, of course, was a last resort as it was assumed that children would support their aged parents until they died.

Two very early instances of centenarian deaths are those of Mary Simons and Elizabeth Tooley. Mary, who was a widow, died in 1622 and it is recorded in Wargrave Register that she was 'about a hundred years old'.

Elizabeth was aged 99, but in her hundredth year, and was buried at Shottesbrooke. Her tomb reads:

Here Lyeth
The Body of ELIZABETH
TOOLEY
Who departed this life Dec br y 2,
1713 aged 99.

Another elderly person who died in his hundreth year was Martin Joseph Routh. Born in 1755 he was the son of a Yorkshire rector and school-master. He became a Fellow of Magdalen before he was twenty and its President at thirty five. He was a fine classical scholar, a keen historian specialising in Stuart times, and a collector of books. When he died it was said he owned 16,000 books.

For three months every year he lived at Tilehurst, where his nephew was curate. He was noted for his quiet politeness and placid nature. The gardener at Tilehurst, who had to be sent away as he had gone mad, begged to be allowed to see Routh before he went. The gardener stooped as if to kiss his hand, but in doing so bit a piece from it.

When Routh was asked how he felt when the man bit his hand he replied: 'Why, at first, Sir, I felt considerably alarmed, for I was unaware what proportion of human virus might have been communicated by the bite; but in the interval of reaching the house I was convinced that the proportion of virus must have been very small indeed; then I was at rest, Sir, but I had the bite cauterized.'

Once, reminded of his approaching end, he replied: 'I am prepared, but I read in the newspapers this morning, Sir, the death of a dissenting minister who has lived to be a hundred and four. I should wish the Church, Sir, to beat Dissent.'

Martin Routh died in 1854 and is buried in the parish churchyard of Tilehurst.

Martha Pye, on the other hand, lived to the ripe old age of 117. She

The grave of Martha Pye, who lived to be 117 years old.

died on April 15 1822 and is buried in All Saints'churchyard, Sutton Courteney. It was said that at the age of 100 Martha walked to Abingdon which is about three miles south-east of Sutton Courtenay – quite a remarkable feat for someone of such an advanced age.

In the churchyard of St Andrew's, East Hagbourne, is the gravestone of Avery Dearlove who, because of the wonderful epitaph, has been included as an 'almost centenarian'.

SACRED
to the Memory of
AVERY DEARLOVE
who died August
the 23rd 1845
in the ninety ninth year of his age
He retained his faculties
to the last and his end
was peace.

A large mansion called Temple House that belonged to the Vansittart family, who also owned Bisham Abbey, was the home and workplace of another centenarian, Ann Green. She had been a housekeeper at Temple House for many years which no doubt had provided her with a good income, comfortable standard of living, and security through savings and a pension.

Distressed gentlewomen, particularly in the last century, were often middle class penniless widows, or single women whose fathers had died or become impoverished – and were

Ann Green's grave at Bisham.

They disciplined and protected staff, sometimes even hiring and dismissing them. Their accommodation, food and drink were all provided together with a salary depending upon their age, range of duties and sometimes even the locality they worked in.

Ann Green must have led a busy, but fulfilling and indeed healthy life to live to the age of 106. She died on February 4, 1862 and is buried in All Saints Parish churchyard, Bisham.

Another grand old Berkshire centenarian was John Faulkner who is buried in St Peter and St Paul churchyard, Appleford. John was a jockey who rode his first winner at the age of eight and his last race at the amazing age of seventy four. He was married twice and had thirty two grandchildren. At the age of ninety he broke his thigh and was told that he would never walk again. Seven weeks later he walked to Abingdon and back, a total of eight miles!

He died on the eve of his 105th birthday in 1933 and at his funeral four black horses drew the wagon containing the coffin to the church.

Even as recently as 1950 the *Berkshire Chronicle,* recording the death of a centenarian, felt that it was still a noteworthy piece of news – 'although some day it may not rank as such, for scientists on the one hand are striving after longevity and on the other hand elaborating fiendish

forced to support themselves. Well-bred ladies lost social status on taking paid employment, but entering a private household as a housekeeper was the least degrading way of earning a living. Some would oversee all the duties carried out in the house, but not mix with the other servants.

They ensured that the complex household ran efficiently, coordinating all the departments. They usually ran the internal economy, ordering, purchasing, storing and distributing goods and keeping careful accounts.

devices to curtail it.'

There is no doubt that the expectancy of life in this century has increased enormously. For Annie Beauchamp Emhurst, who was born in 1849, and died on June 5, 1950, a lifetime of 101 years was a fine achievement.

Her father was a captain in the Royal Navy and many of the trophies he brought home from his travels are now in the Royal Naval Museum at Greenwich. In her younger years Annie travelled all over the world. She remained active until her ninetieth year, when she broke a leg. Gradually she became an invalid and for the last two years of her life was confined to her room. No doubt her hobbies of music and painting were of comfort to her in those last few years. Her gravestone is to be found in St Peter's churchyard, Earley.

Catherine Bramwell-Booth, granddaughter of the founder of the Salvation Army, was born in 1883 and lived until her 105th year. She died on October 3, 1987. Catherine worked tirelessly as a Commissioner in the Salvation Army and had been retired for almost thirty years, living peacefully with her mother and sisters in their large house in Finchampstead, Berkshire, when suddenly her life took a new twist.

The BBC telephoned and asked her to do an interview on television and the response created new work for Catherine. Her vivid personality, her sense of fun and her humorous kind of spirituality endeared her to people everywhere. Broadcasters like Michael Parkinson and Russell Harty were astounded at this little old lady's ability to master the media. In 1978 Commissioner Catherine CBE received a somewhat incongruous award. She was elected Best Speaker of the Year by the Guild of Professional Toastmasters.

Even though Catherine had been born into an age when the letter and telegram were the fastest means of communication, and radio and television had yet to be invented, she could, in her 100th year, effortlessly master a medium undreamt of in her youth. She could hold a television or radio audience in the way that her grandfather had held the attention of a public meeting. She used charm and humour but was not afraid to speak her mind.

Catherine Bramwell-Booth was a truly remarkable woman. She is buried with the rest of her family in the churchyard of St James' Church, Finchampstead. The epitaph at the bottom of the tomb reads:

Daughters
of General and Mrs Bramwell-Booth
of the Salvation Army.
These all lived and died Trusting
Jesus.
HE EVER LIVETH.

Other epitaphs to centenarians

In memory of Thomas Anns
who died Nov 30 1767
aged 54 years
Alfo Martha his wife who died
Aug 10 1802
aged 100 years.
They reft in hope exerupt
from pain
They live to Christ
Their deaths are gain.
St Augustine, East Hendred

SOPHIA BUCKLAND
AGED 100
On a small wooden cross in the
churchyard at Bracknell.

Inside the parish church of West
Hannay an epitaph is recorded of
Elizabeth Bowles, who died at the
age of 124, year of death unknown.

CHILDREN

MANY gravestones in Berkshire churchyards record the appalling infant mortality of the eighteenth and nineteenth centuries. Even the simplest of epitaphs, giving only names and dates, bear testimony to the loss experienced by so many parents of at least one child, sometimes many more.

Today families tend to be much smaller, but right up until the beginning of this century and beyond, ten or even up to twenty children was not uncommon for parents to bring into the world. It was rare for all these children to survive and many died from illnesses unknown today.

Many babies died soon after birth, having had little nourishment whilst in the womb, let alone in the world once it was born. Baptism took place soon after birth for there was always the possibility that a baby might survive for only a few hours or days.

Infant mortality deaths did not begin to decline until the beginning of this century.

In poorer families births were usually two years apart because mothers were breast feeding their infants. Among the upper classes, where the use of wet-nurses was common, births were more frequent. It seemed that most parents felt it was best to bring as many children into the world as possible for few of them might live. Yet less frequent childbearing might have been far better for the health not only of the mother, but also of the children themselves.

The baby who survived the trials of birth faced many other dangers apart from the high risk of childhood disease. There were the physical dangers present in small, cluttered homes, for often safety precautions were ignored or not thought about. Also many babies had no cradles and slept in their mothers' beds, thus running the risk of suffocation.

In a world which knew nothing of antibiotics and little of innoculation, children were at risk from pneumonia, rheumatic fever, scarlet fever, measles, diphtheria, smallpox, whooping cough – the list was endless.

In poorer families the children were often sent out to work at the age of six or seven and could literally die from overwork, hunger or illnesses brought on by constant hardship. An investigation that took place in 1908 revealed that almost ten per cent of the country's two million school children worked outside school hours – a figure which, high though it was, excluded half-timers, street traders and perhaps beggars and petty criminals.

Unhealthy children grew into unhealthy adults. Some of the diseases they contracted may not have been fatal, but could result in lifelong problems and so the cycle of deprivation continued.

Attitudes to childhood deaths was not exactly casual, but expected. Even so their grief must have been shocking to bear and the poignant epitaphs reflect the pain these deaths must have caused the parents. Very often the baby would be referred to as an angel or a bud in lines such as:

This lovely bud so young and fair
Called home to early doom.

The youngest recorded death accompanied by the briefest of epitaphs was that for Charles Payton. Buried in St Peter's churchyard, Earley, he lived for one minute and was buried in an unmarked grave on May 1, 1905.

Alfred Blayney Handasyd lived only a little longer. He died aged seven weeks on March 30, 1780, but he was given a most majestic little tomb close to the side of the road at St Nicholas' churchyard, Hurst.

An equally majestic square tomb, with a Latin inscription, stands in front of the porch door of St Michael the Archangel, Warfield. It is inscribed to Sarah Skelton, who died in 1751, aged fifteen. Her father, Thomas Skelton was not only the Vicar of Warfield, but the first Headmaster of Warfield Preparatory School.

Sarah died only a year after the family arrived in Warfield and was

The tomb of fifteen year old
Sarah Skelton.

buried standing up – it was said that she had been a very good dancer and was, therefore, buried in an eternal pirouette.

On visiting St Mary's Church, Shinfield, it is hard not to be moved by the poignant story told in a wall plaque to the memory of the Wilder children. The plaque records:

Near this Place
Lies interred
Francis Phillips Wilder
2nd Son
of Lieut.Col. Wilder
of this Parish
who died the 10th of Dec 1797
Aged 3 weeks

Francis John Phillips Wilder
who died the 30th April 1800
Aged 3 Months
Henry Phillips Wilder
who died the 13th July 1801
Aged 3 Weeks
Henry Phillips Wilder
who died the 17th January 1808
Aged 13 Days.

It is impossible not to notice that the parents named two children Francis and two children Henry – still losing all of them.

It appears from another plaque that the same family lost another son called Francis who had reached the age of fourteen when he fell from the East India Company's Ship *Astell* into the Bay of Bengal and drowned on September 24, 1816. His father, who by then was a Major General, died soon after losing his son.

There is something infinitely poignant about a gravestone for twins and although the one at the Church of St Mary the Virgin, Hurley, is rather solid and forbidding, it bears the sweetest of epitaphs:

In Memory of
JOSIAH and BENJAMIN
JAMES MASON,
Infant Sons of
JOSEPH & MARY MASON
who died March 7th 1819
Aged 5 Weeks
Here lies two Pure
and footlefs Babes;
As parents e'er could

The grave of tragic twins Josiah and Benjamin Mason.

Wifh to have,
Their Days were fhort,
Complaint fevere
Which fnatch'd them from
their Parents dear.
But God on them had fix'd his Love
And took them to the Realms above.

John Alfred and Thomas Hubert Smith lived for only ten weeks and died on October 15, 1810. They are buried in the prettiest of churchyards belonging to Waltham St Lawrence.

Sleep little babies
in your beds below
let the wild flowers

shroud you
let the rain drops
bathe you
let the sun's rays warm you
till we hold you once more
at Heaven's door.

And what of the parents who lost all their children at the same time from one of the dreaded diseases so prevalent in the 1800s?

Two such families can be found in Berkshire. The first is in the church-yard of St Deny's, Stanford-in-the Vale. Here is the grave of shopkeep-ers Charles and Mary Goulding's five children who all died together. The epitaph reads:

IN MEMORY OF

CHARLES, JOHN

MARY, HARRIET

AND ANN

SONS AND DAUGHTERS

OF CHARLES AND

MARY GOULDING

WHO DIED IN THE AUTUMN

OF THE YEAR 1841

OF TYPHUS FEVER.

SUFFER LITTLE CHILDREN

TO COME UNTO ME ,

OF SUCH IS THE KINGDOM

OF HEAVEN.

There is a story about this church-yard at Stanford-in-the-Vale of a ghost. It is said that sometimes at night a grey lady can be seen flitting around the gravestones. However, no one seems to know who she might be.

Charles and Mary Goulding lost all five of their children .

The second family not only lost all their children, but their own lives as well. The entire family died of fever within the space of three months. Their gravestone can be found at Clifton Hampden in the churchyard of St Michael.

IN MEMORY OF

JOHN GLANVILL

AND SARAH, HIS WIFE

AND THREE OF THEIR CHILDREN

WHO ALL DIED OF FEVER

WITHIN A SHORT TIME OF

ONE ANOTHER

HE DIED 14TH SEPT R 1865

AGED 55 YEARS

SHE DIED 16TH AUG ST 1965

The Glanvills – parents John and Sarah, and all three of their children died within three months.

ARTHUR CHARLES
THE BELOVED SON OF
ARTHUR CHARLES AND
LUCY SNUGGS
OF NEW WINDSOR
WHO DIED MARCH 15TH 1857
AGED ONE YEAR AND EIGHT MONTHS
OF SUCH IS THE KINGDOM OF HEAVEN
ALSO OF
LOUISA, THE BELOVED DAUGHTER
OF THE ABOVE
WHO DIED MAY 2ND 1860
IN THE EIGHTH MONTH OF HER AGE
ALSO OF FREDERICK JOHN
SON OF THE ABOVE
WHO DIED DECEMBER 3RD 1861
AGED 8 MONTHS

AGED 48 YEARS
OF THEIR CHILDREN
LOUISA GLANVILL DIED 15TH SEPT R
1865 AGED 15 YEARS
JOHN SAWYER GLANVILL DIED 13TH SEPT
1865 AGED 17 YEARS
HENRY POULTON GLANVILLE DIED 8 OCT
1865 AGED 7 YEARS
WATCH THEREFORE FOR YE KNOW NOT
WHAT HOUR YOUR LORD DOTH COME.

A gravestone in the name of Snuggs, in the churchyard at St Peter and St Andrew, Old Windsor, records the death of three children, none of whom reached the age of two.

IN REMEMBRANCE OF

The three infant Snuggs children are buried in this Windsor grave.

Mary Humfrey's simple stone.

Harry Marshall's cross.

Baby Harry Marshall 'fell asleep' (a phrase that occurs again and again in children's and adult's epitaphs) on June 22, 1872, aged ten months. His cross memorial in St Mary's churchyard, Wargrave, remembers him with affection.

Mary Humfrey lived only five days and is buried in St Mary's churchyard, White Waltham. Although the headstone is fairly plain it is softened by the wild rose clinging to one side of it and the daisies nestling at its feet.

SACRED

TO THE MEMORY OF

MARY

INFANT DAUGHTER OF

EDWARD AND CAROLINE HUMFREY

BORN OCT.25.1872

DIED OCT.30.1872

Hidden beneath trails of clinging ivy, crouching behind a holly tree is the small stone cross in memory of Walter and Flora Stiff, two beloved children who are buried in St Mary's churchyard, Shinfield.

IN

AFFECTIONATE

REMEMBRANCE

OF WALTER HORATIO STIFF

WHO DIED JANUARY 22:1880

AGED 1 YEAR & 2 MONTHS

ALSO

FLORA KATE STIFF

WHO DIED JULY 15:1886

AGED 5 YEARS & 6 MONTHS.

PEACE, LOVE, LITTLE SLEEPERS
CLOSE TO THY SAVIOUR'S SIDE.
The parents of Alice and Daniel Waters suffered two tragedies within three years. When they lost Alice perhaps they had prayed to be allowed to keep Daniel, but it was not to be.
Both children are buried in St Mary's churchyard, Kintbury.

To the Memory of
ALICE DAISY WATERS
WHO DIED NOV. 29th 1879
AGED 18 MONTHS
ALSO OF
DANIEL HENRY WATERS
BROTHER OF THE ABOVE
WHO DIED APRIL 13th 1882
AGED 10 YEARS.

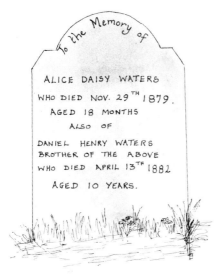

Baby Alice Waters, and her ten year old brother Daniel.

A grand gravestone for young Taddy Caulfeild.

In St Andrew's churchyard, Bradfield, is a most unusual memorial situated close to a very tall yew hedge. The epitaph reads:

IN LOVING MEMORY OF
S.N. ST G CAULFEILD
'TADDY'
YOUNGEST SON OF
FRANCIS ST GEORGE CAULFEILD
Died Oct. 25th 1898
Aged 13 years.

An explanation for this young boy's death is to be found in an obituary from *The Bradfield College Chronicle* dated October 1898 –

although the date and age in the obituary are quoted differently from that recorded on the gravestone.

'On October 26th, at Bradfield, Stewart Neil St George Caulfeild, aged 14 . . . a member of the family well-known to Bradfield boys, entered the Junior School in September 1894, and gained his Remove into the Army House as lately as September in this year. His very short illness with its sudden and fatal termination, though due to causes apart from our School life, has cast a gloom over the whole community, and the sympathies of all connected with the College have gone out towards the bereaved family.'

Another boy who died young was Maurice Spagnolettio. Apparently this ten year old died suddenly in London, but his home must have been in Pangbourne, for he is buried in St James the Less's churchyard, with a most elaborate headstone as his memorial. Maurice was born on February 10, 1906, and died on June 8, 1916.

The headstone, although large, would be easy to miss as it is hidden away beneath undergrowth to one side of the church.

On a glorious summer day Peggy Cotesworth Bond's headstone stood out from right across the other side of the churchyard of St Mary's, Wargrave.

With the fir trees' shadows dap-

Peggy Cotesworth Bond's grave

pling the sculpture of a young girl inset into the stone, it was impossible to miss.

The epitaph reads:

IN MEMORY

OF PEGGY

*only daughter of William Cotesworth
& Greta Bond
born 23rd January 1909
died
18th January 1913.*

Although it does not say so on Peggy's gravestone, on one nearby the epitaph makes it clear that

An angel clutches the cross on two year old Bridget Cooney's grave

*In Memory of HENRY son of Joseph & Martha Hopkins,who departed this life April 10th 1748."
In Memory of SARAH, daughter of Joseph & Martha Hopkins, who departed this life Sept. 25th 1751.*
Double boy and girl stone at St Mary, Cholsey.

William and Greta were married, using the surname Cotesworth Bond.

The final epitaph chosen from all the children buried in Berkshire's churchyards is that of Bridget Camilla Cooney, who died in March, 1933. Her headstone is to be found in the additional churchyard belonging to St Michael the Archangel, Warfield, which is across the road from the church. There is an angel easily the size of a small child, resting against a plain white cross at whose feet lies a teddy bear covered in moss and lichen. It says:

BRIDGET CAMILLA COONEY
BORN OCTOBER 1,1930
DIED MARCH 3 1933.

*To Perpetuate the memory of MARTHA MURRAY daughter of Michael and Isabella Murray, who died May the 31st 1792 Aged 16 Years.
One of the most lovely of her sex she was, tho'
less conspicuous for her tender and sincere affection as a daughter than for her strict attention to her family
as a sister: she died regretted by all her friends, and her loss is most felt by her disconsolate parents.*
St Andrew, Clewer.

To Perpetuate
while this frail
memorial shall endure
the memory
of Mary FOREMAN
who died on the 21 day of Feb. 1817
at the age of 15 years, after a
lingering illness which she
bore with exemplary fortitude.
Scarce had her
blossom....the dew
Or felt the suns broad day
When from the north the wild blast came
And swept the flower away.
So fell my child's life's gloomy foe
His fatal arrow sped
The object of my fondest hopes
Was numbered with the dead.
St Mary, Longcott.

SACRED

TO THE MEMORY OF

CHARLES HODGES

WHO DIED OCTOBER 19TH 1842

AFTER A FEW DAYS ILLNESS

IN THE 11th YEAR OF HIS AGE.
The spring of life had scarce begun
'Ere he his mortal race had run,
So good a boy, beloved by all,
Regret not friends his early call.
St Mary the Virgin, Hurley.

FROGMORE

THE Frogmore estate first came into royal ownership in the mid-sixteenth century, but it was held by a succession of Crown tenants for the following 250 years. It formed a substantial enclave between the Great Park and Home park of Windsor, and no doubt it was the close proximity of the estate to Windsor Castle that prompted its purchase by the Crown.

In May 1841 Queen Victoria, who had ascended the throne in 1837, asked her widowed mother, the Duchess of Kent, if she would like to use Frogmore House and its pleasure grounds as her country home. The Duchess lived at Frogmore for much of the following twenty years and when she died in March, 1861, her body was laid to rest in her own mausoleum in the grounds. This building, on a mound above the Swiss Seat,

between two arms of the lake, replaced an octagonal gothic Temple of Solitude which had stood there until the 1850s.

The Duchess of Kent Mauseoleum is a small circular building, surrounded by columns with an upper chamber occupied by a full-length statue of the Duchess, and a lower burial chamber containing her sacophagus. Work began on the building in the late 1850s under the direction of Prince Albert, Queen Victoria's husband. The upper level of the building was intended to serve as a summer house during the Duchess's lifetime, but work was still under way at the time of her death, so her statue was laid there instead. This building is not open to the public.

Close to the steps of the Duchess of Kent Mausoleum, just over a bridge spanning one of the canals leading from the lake, is a memorial cross to Lady Augusta Stanley, who

The Duchess of Kent Mausoleum at Frogmore.

was a devoted friend and servant to both the Duchess and Queen Victoria. The inscription reads:

TO THE DEAR MEMORY

OF

LADY AUGUSTA LEY

5th DAUGHTER OF THOMAS BRUCE

7th EARL OF ELGIN AND KINCARDINE.

THIS CROSS IS ERECTED

BY QUEEN VICTORIA

IN GRATEFUL AND

AFFECTIONATE REMEMBRANCE

OF HER FAITHFUL LABOURS

FOR 30 YEARS

IN THE SERVICE OF THE QUEEN

THE DUCHESS OF KENT

AND THE ROYAL FAMILY.

BORN APRIL 3, 1822

DIED MARCH 1,1876.

Although the flat natural setting at Frogmore did not commend itself for the creation of a garden, the extensive grounds to the west of Frogmore House have provided the chief and enduring attraction of Frogmore to the Royal Family. Once the adjoining estate of Great Frogmore had been included the grounds totalled nearly thirty five acres. The grounds were maintained and greatly appreciated by the Duchess of Kent and indeed the gardens at Frogmore remained especially sacred for Queen Victoria, who came to the throne, aged eighteen, in 1837, and the Royal Family.

As early as 1843, Queen Victoria and Prince Albert, who had married on February 10, 1840, had agreed not

Queen Victoria's cross for Lady Augusta Ley.

to be buried in the royal vault in St. George's Chapel, but in a mauseoleum specially designed for them.

Prince Albert declared a wish to be buried in Queen Charlotte's garden in the grounds of Frogmore.

He died on December 14, 1861, at the age of forty two, from typhoid fever, his illness having lasted two weeks.

Four days after Prince Albert died the Queen chose the site for their mauseoleum in the south west end of the garden. The building was to take the form of a cross, with a central octagonal chamber covered with a dome, inspired by Italian Romanesque buildings, while the ornamentation of the interior employed the style of the Italian Renaissance painter Raphael, considered by Prince Albert to be the greatest painter of all time.

On the December 17, 1862, the unfinished mauseoleum was consecrated, and early next morning the

The Victoria and Albert Mausoleum at Frogmore.

Princes' body was removed from St George's Chapel, where it had lain in the entrance to the royal vault, and taken to a temporary sarcophagus at Frogmore.

The building took another six years to complete. Queen Victoria wanted it to be a memorial of her husband's interest in the natural products of the world, so materials were obtained from many lands. The woodwork was of Indian teak; the roof of Australian copper; there were marbles from Wales and Scotland; the Channel Islands and Scotland supplied the granite; Portland stone came from England; and further marble was sent from Belgium, France, Italy, Greece and Portugal.

The great dome represented a blue night sky strewn with golden stars and held aloft by gilded angels. Immediately below this was placed the Prince's tomb, designed by Baron Marochetti. The sarcophagus was a double one, made from a complete block of dark grey Aberdeen granite; it was said to be the largest flawless block of granite in existence. The plinth of polished black marble was a gift from Leopold I of the Belgians. At each corner of the tomb knelt a bronze angel with wings outstretched.

On the December 26, 1868, the Prince was laid in the tomb and upon it his recumbent statue in white marble was placed – Baron Marochetti's last work before his own death earlier that year. He had already made a similar statue of Queen Victoria so that when it was required it would match that of the Prince.

The epitaph on Prince Albert's side of the tomb reads:

FRANCIS ALBERT AUGUSTUS
CHARLES EMANUEL
DUKE OF SAXONY: PRINCE OF
SAXE-COBURG & GOTHA
PRINCE CONSORT
SECOND SON OF ERNEST
REIGNING DUKE OF
SAXE-COBURG AND GOTHA
BORN AT THE ROSEN AU NEAR COBURG
AUG: 26: 1819
MARRIED FEB: 10: 1840
TO VICTORIA QUEEN OF ENGLAND
AND IRELAND
DIED WINDSOR DEC: 14: 1861.

Throughout the forty years of her widowhood, Queen Victoria always observed the anniversary of her husbands' death. She laid fresh flowers on the Prince's deathbed and knelt in prayer beside it before she and the other members of the family attended a memorial service in the mausoleum.

Only once was this service cancelled – on the very the morning of the anniversary of Prince Albert's death, when his second daughter, Alice, Grand Duchess of Hesse, died at Darmstadt in 1878. She had contracted diphtheria while nursing her husband and children. Her four year old daughter, Princess May, had died the month before from the same disease.

Quen Victoria commanded Sir Edgar Boehm to build a memorial in the form of a statue of the Grand Duchess in the mausoleum. Alice lies upon a marble tomb clasping to her side the figure of the child she had nursed so lovingly, her head supported by angels while her cloak drapes over the end of her feet. On one side are the words:

To the Memory of my much loved and
lamented Daughter
ALICE, Grand Duchess of HESSE
who survived but a few Days the
fever stricken Child beside whom
SHE had watched not
counting HER life dear to HERSELF.

Queen Victoria died at Osborne, her small estate on the Isle of Wight, on January 22, 1901. Hers had been the longest reign of a monarch in English history. After a procession by sea and land her body reached Windsor for burial on Saturday, February 2, the final part of the journey having been completed by train.

At Windsor Station a Royal Artillery gun carriage drawn by horses, waited to bear her body to St George's Chapel.

The coffin was covered by a white satin pall and surmounted by the regalia and insignia of the Garter.

Either because of the drum rolls, firing of cannons or the intense cold, one of the horses on the off-side nearest to the wagon suddenly became uneasy. The driver was unable to control him and the horse lashed out, catching one of his hind legs in the pole-bar, and he fell on his knees.

It was decided for safety's sake to remove all the horses and to replace them with the Blue Jackets forming a guard of honour. So sailors in blue uniforms and straw hats pulled the gun carriage through the hushed streets, while the Curfew and Round Tower bells tolled.

It is because of this unrehearsed incident that Englands' sovereigns are now always drawn by sailors at their burials.

After the funeral service Queen Victoria's body was laid in the Albert Memorial Chapel and then on Monday, February 4, to the renewed tolling of the two big bells, it was borne to Frogmore to be interred with the Princes' body. Her epitaph reads:

VICTORIA

QUEEN OF GREAT BRITAIN & IRELAND:

EMPRESS OF INDIA

BORN AT KENSINGTON PALACE

24 MAY 1819;

SUCCEEDED 20 JUNE, 1837:

DIED AT OSBORNE 22 JANUARY 1901.

Just below this is a silver cross lying across a Union Flag pillow surrounded by oak leaves and fruits, with these words:

PEACE PERFECT PEACE

OUR LOVED ONES FAR AWAY

IN JESUS' KEEPING

Another view of the Victoria and Albert Mausoleum at Frogmore.

WE ARE SAFE AND THEY

HOW WE MISS THAT WELCOME VOICE

HOW WE MARK THAT VACANT CHAIR

FOR THE LOVED ONE TAKEN FROM US

SEEMS THE ONE WE LEAST CAN SPARE.

FOR QUEEN VICTORIA FROM HER EVER

GRATEFUL AND LOVING

DAUGHTER-IN-LAW, ALEXANDRA.

The area to the south west of the Royal Mausoleum was consecrated for use as a private burial ground in 1928. It ís dominated by a vast figure of Christ by the Swedish sculptor Laurits Rasmussen, which was presented by Queen Alexandra in 1903 as a 'tribute of love and affection to the best and greatest of Sovereigns and the kindest of mothers-in-law, from her ever grateful and most loving daughter-in-law, Alexandra.'

Among those buried there are three of Queen Victoria's children: Princess Helena and her husband Prince Christian; Prince Arthur, Duke of Connaught with his wife, and Princess Louise. In more recent times, Prince William of Gloucester and Princess Alice, Countess of Athlone have also been buried there.

This private burial ground is closed to the public, but across the grass in the far corner close to the yew hedge are the memorials to the Duke and Duchess of Windsor.

The heir to the throne had met the twice-married American, Wallis Simpson, in July 1931 and had fallen in love. When George V died on January 20, 1936, the prince succeeded, as Edward VIII. He felt the only obstacle to a lifetime of happiness with Wallis was her husband, Ernest.

The new King persuaded a reluctant Ernest to provide grounds for a divorce, and in return he promised to protect Wallis for the rest of her life.

But a divorced woman was not acceptable to the court or to the British public, and the King said that if he could not marry the woman he loved, then he would abdicate.

So, on Thursday, December 10, 1936, Edward signed an Instrument of Abdication. That night, after the ex-king made his celebrated farewell broadcast, telling the world that he had found it 'impossible to do my duty as King and Emperor without

The Duke and Duchess of Windsor are buried beneath the shade of this great plane tree.

the help and support of the woman I love', he left for France as the Duke of Windsor. The Duke married Wallis on June 3, 1937, in France.

The Duke, a heavy smoker, became ill early in 1972, and died of cancer of the larynx on May 28, 1972.

Some years earlier the Royal Family had discovered that the Windsors had purchased a burial plot in Baltimore. This caused widespread dismay in Britain and the Queen agreed to their being buried together in a private mausoleum in the grounds of Frogmore.

A few years later the Duke asked

if they might be buried not in a mausoleum, but in the Royal Family's own burial ground nearby, and the Queen agreed.

The Duke was interred at Frogmore beneath the shade of a great plane tree with the simple words:

EDWARD, DUKE OF WINDSOR
1894 – 1972

The Duchess noticed that the space reserved for herself seemed very small, and remarked upon it. As a result the hedge was moved further back to make room for her burial spot when the time came.

Just before Christmas in that same year, 1972, the Duchess suffered a bad fall and broke her hip – the first of several such accidents. On November 13, 1975, she suffered a massive intestinal heamorrhage and it was thought that she was dying. However, she received devoted care from her butler Georges and his wife, and she lived for another ten years.

The Duchess died on the April 24, 1986, a few weeks short of her ninetieth birthday. Her remains were flown to Britain and following a funeral service at St George's Chapel, Windsor, when apparently her name was not mentioned once, she was interred next to her husband in the burial ground at Frogmore, again with the simple epitaph:

WALLIS, Duchess of Windsor.
19 June 1896 – 1986.

Frogmore House, the Royal Mausoleum and gardens can be visited for only two days each year during the month of May.

HUSBANDS AND WIVES

UNTIL well into this century marriages were based less upon romantic love and sexual satisfaction than upon a sense of companionship and the need to procreate.

Companiable marriages had always existed but as people's living conditions improved and the size of families reduced, husbands and wives had more time for each other and were able to enjoy each other's company.

This was particularly true for the better off who did not have to spend time arguing with one another about money.

The churchyards of Berkshire have their fair share of epitaphs which tell us of the love and caring shared by many couples down through the centuries. Sometimes the actual gravestone symbolises that even in death a husband and wife cannot be parted.

Such is the case for Will and Elizabeth Bristow, whose headstone can be found in the churchyard at St Mary the Virgin, Burghfield. The exact dates of their passing are uncertain, but they lived to the ages of eighty two and seventy seven respectively. It is the oldest tomb in the churchyard and the double headstones are joined together to show that even in death Will and Elizabeth were not divided.

An epitaph to be found in St Bartholomew, Arborfield is simple and stately:

MRS ANN COOK
Relict of MR WILLIAM COOK
who had died aged 51 in 1751
followed her honored Hufband
into Eternal Blifs
upon the 18th day of February 1789
in the 86 Year of her Age.

A plaque to John and Rebecca Webster can be found at St Mary's, Shinfield, which by the way has six bells. This is mentioned purely because of what is written on the last three bells, which were put in the tower in 1722 and are inscribed:

Churchwardens Daniel Headland,
Thomas Hollyer, Henry Bagley
made mee 1722.

John Webster, was a citizen of London, but in 1737 with his wife Rebecca, he bought a little farm on the edge of Shinfield Common. They developed it into an estate planting many trees – especially oaks – alongside the road bordering their land. They lived there for many years and on their deaths passed the estate to their four children. Rebecca died first in 1785 and her epitaph reads:

This day I died,
tomorrow you muft go
You know not where,
In hope e'er now I know.

Seven years later John joined her in death with the words:

Open the grave my promise
firm to keep
We both agreed
together here to sleep
In bonds of friendship
as we lived we died
To ever lasting rest lay side by side.

Epitaphs like this were not unusual during the last few centuries. Flowery, sentimental verses adorned many headstones whether for a man, woman or child. Nowadays they appear out of fashion and in some cases overwhelming, but they reflected the feelings of the people at that time and when read whilst wandering around a churchyard they come across as beautiful and quite often most moving.

One husband's death was recorded on his gravestone in a manner sometimes adopted two or more centuries ago when the craftsman writing the epitaph would split words and go on to the next line no matter what word he was working on. In Childrey parish churchyard is just such a headstone which reads:

Here lieth the
body of Thomas
Allen the Hus
band of Jane Al
len who was
buried Septem
ber the
9 day
1678
Aged 53.

Two instances of married couples dying on the same day are to be found in Berkshire.

In St Michael's churchyard, Lambourn, is the gravestone for Thomas and Joane Stiffe:

HERE LYETH BODY of
THOMAS
SON OF THOMAS STIFFE
AND JOANE HIS WIFE
DAUGHTER OF THOMAS BRUNSDON
WHO DIED IN 67th YEAR OF HIS AGE
AND 58th YEAR OF HER AGE
AND WERE BURIED BOTH TOGETHER
IN ONE GRAVE
ON 25 DAY OF JUNE 1700

John and Jane Blacknall died on the same day some seventy five years earlier than Thomas and Joane on August 21, 1625, apparently from the plague.

John Blacknall was born in 1583. Educated at the Free School, Queens College, Oxford and at the Middle Temple, was called to the Bar. He was a leading man in the county in terms of wealth and position, marrying into the Blagrove family. The couple are buried at St Nicholas, Abingdon and their monument, which was not erected until 1684, was mentioned in the book *Three Men in a Boat*, although the name was given as Blackwall, not Blacknall. Part of the poem on their monument in the church reads:

When once they liv'd on earth one
bed did hold

*Their bodies which one minute turn'd
to mould
Being dead, one grave is trusted with
that prize
Until the trump doth sound and all
must rise
Here death's stroke even did not part
this pair,
But by this stroke they more united
were.*

There is also evidence of couples who died within days of one another. Only twelve hours separated the deaths of Mr and Mrs William James Morten. The husband, aged sixty seven, was returning from working at Rayners Farm, Slough, when he dropped dead. His wife, who had been seriously ill for some time, died twelve hours later. They were buried together on January 22, 1933.

Ten years later Charles Russell caught pneumonia and died in December, 1943, aged eighty three. His wife, who had been an invalid for many years and was eighty two , died the following day.

Charles Russell was the second son of Henry Russell who had been known as 'the grand old man of Reading', and had been chairman of the Reading Philanthropic Institution for many years.

The Russell's funeral took place at All Saints, Reading.

Three days separated Jane Collins from joining her husband William in

**William and Jane Collins died
within three days of each other.**

May 1882. Their gravestone can be found near the church porch in St Peter's churchyard, Cranbourne, and shows that they were married for fifty three years.

IN

*Affectionate
Remembrance
of*
*WILLIAM COLLINS
AGED 81 YEARS
ALSO
JANE HIS WIFE
AGED 85 YEARS
WHO DIED MAY 1882
IN LIFE TOGETHER 53 YEARS
SEPARATED BY DEATH 3 DAYS*

Another couple who were married for many years were William and Elizabeth Smith. Their gravestone can be seen in the churchyard of St Mary's, Shinfield. Elizabeth died on June 28, 1846, aged seventy four and her husband died the following February, 1847, aged seventy three. An epitaph says:

All that is mortal of our Parents
dear
Overwhelm'd with sorrow
we deposit here.
But now O Grave thy
territories strong
Shall not detain the friends
we grieve for long.
When a few rolling seasons
more are gone
When that bright day
which ne'er shall close dawn
They'll rise again with
renovated powers
And soars aloft to Heavens
perennial bowers
To share in those serene
retreats above,
The pleasures
purchas'd with a Saviours love,
For in their conduct all
their neighbours round
Through their long course a bright
example found.
They the straight paths of virtue
strictly trod
Did justly, and walk'd humbly with
their God.

The joint headstone of Richard and Faith Pearce.

Another eloquent epitaph records the deaths of Richard and Faith Pearce who share a joined headstone in St Andrew's churchyard, Sonning. Richard died first on May 26, 1800, aged seventy eight years, with the words:

Free from Malice
void of pride,
So he liv'd and fo he Died;
Remember me
tho' I am gone,
A friend to all a foe to none.

His wife, Faith, died two months later on the July 30, aged seventy five years. Her epitaph reads:

Oft as the bell, with folemn toll,
Speakes the departure of a foul;
Let each one afk himfelf, Am I
Prepar'd fhould I be called to die.

The gravestone of Elizabeth Sadgrave is to be seen in St Nicholas's churchyard, Hurst.

Elizabeth and Moses Sadgrave lie here in Hurst churchyard.

HERE
hath Interr'd the Body of
Mrs ELIZABETH SADGRAVE
Late Wife of
Mr MOSES SADGRAVE
Late of this Parifh
who departed
this life
the 26th day of April 1767
In the 78th Year
of her Age
This monumental Stone
is erected by THOMAS ELLIS.

Benjamin Beaver obviously regarded his wife with a great deal of love and respect for he erected a

The Beaver tomb at Wokingham, records the deaths of some sixty members of the family.

huge rectangular tomb made from Portland stone to her memory in All Saints' churchyard, Wokingham. The inscription for Elizabeth Beaver, who died in 1787, says:

ERECTED FOR THE LASTING
REMEMBRANCE
OF ONE OF THE BEST WOMEN
WHO DESERVED
MORE THAN I CAN SAY OF HER AND FOR
WHOSE SAKE I HAVE ENGAGED PART OF
MY ESTATE TO KEEP UP THIS MONUMENT
IN REPAIR TO THE END OF TIME.

On the same side, but twenty six years previously, it records the death of the Beavers' nephew, Thomas Leach, who had drowned, aged sixteen, whilst swimming near Caversham Lock. Between 1785 ands 1789 Benjamin Beaver filled in the remainder of this monument by researching his family history from

Although provision was made for the upkeep of the Mollony tomb at All Saints, Wokingham, it is now in a sad state of decay.

the time of Charles I to the late eighteenth century. Although disputes still linger as to whether all the inscriptions are correct, it is believed that there are about sixty other relatives mentioned on this tomb.

The churchyard at All Saints, Wokingham, has another large monument in need of repair, to the memory of Daniel and Elizabeth Mollony. On the side it says:

DANIEL MOLLONY

APRIL 11, 1839.

ELIZABETH MARY MOLLONY

MAY 13, 1857.

In her Will, which was proved on July l4, 1857, Elizabeth Mollony left £150 to the vicar and churchwardens;

the dividends were to be used for keeping the tomb in repair. The surplus not required for this purpose was supposed to be divided equally between the old women in the almshouses near the church at Wokingham. Until this century it was thought that the Will had been carried out by United Charities who had taken over the responsibility and made the gift to the women in the almshouses each Christmas.

However, investigations by the present vicar seem to reveal no trace of this bequest now and, judging by the state of the Mollony tomb, this seems to be the case..

Epitaphs from loving wives to

their departed husbands are easily found in Berkshire churchyards. One such is at All Saints, Bisham. Elizabeth Rolls managed to convey everything she must have felt at that sad time:

Sacred to the Memory of
JOHN ROLLS
of Great Marlow,
Who after a Life spent in the
midst of domestic happinefs
and in the practice of
universal kindnefs,
Died on the 8th of October 1820,
in the 70th Year of his Age,
Leaving an afflicted Widow:
and nine gratefully attach'd
Children who have consecrated
this Stone to his memory.

Some fourteen years later Elizabeth herself died and no doubt their nine children added this epitaph:

Also to the Memory of
ELIZABETH, His Wife
who after pafsing a Life,
of peace and usefulnefs in
the bosom of an affectionate
Family died December 31st 1834,
Aged 83 Years.

George Quelch's widow must have felt equally distraught to judge by the beautifully carved gravestone at St Peter, Woolhampton:

IN MEMORY
OF GEORGE QUELCH
WHO DIED OCT: 15.1873 AGED 52.
THE CUP WAS BITTER THE TRIAL SEVERE
TO PART WITH A HUSBAND I LOVED
SO DEAR
MY TRIALS WERE GREAT, I MUST
NOT COMPLAIN
BUT TRUST IN CHRIST TO MEET AGAIN.

The name Pither crops up in churchyards across Berkshire. In St Michael's, Sunninghill it is William Pither who is remembered by his wife – another Elizabeth, one of the most common Christian names found on gravestones. From the tone of the epitaph it could be that William suffered for a while before dying and his wife's regret at his death was tinged with relief at his release from further suffering.

IN LOVING REMEMBRANCE
OF
WILLIAM PITHER
WHO DIED PEACEFULLY

George Quelch, Woolhampton.

The Pither headstone.

*A faithful husband and
sincere friend.
Happy Spirit thou art blest,
Thou hast entered into
rest,
Freed from earth, released
from pain
Thou hast proved to die is
gain.*

As in so many other cases, the children added their own epitaph for their mother who died in 1887, aged seventy one years.

*ALSO IN LOVING
REMEMBRANCE
of ELIZABETH PTTHER
WIDOW OF THE ABOVE
Who passed away to heaven
June 16-1887.*

*AGED 71 YEARS.
A beloved, devoted and
tender Mother.
Jesus gently called His loved
one to Him
I come, her dying looks replied
And lamb-like as her Lord she died.*

The gravestones of Sarah and Caleb Gould are in the pretty churchyard of St Nicholas, Remenham Hill, on a hill close to the River Thames and the boundary crossing to Oxfordshire.

Both headstones have wonderful epitaphs. Sarah died first in 1813:

*To the Memory of SARAH
the Wife of
CALEB GOULD
who Died October 18th 1813
Aged 69 Years.
Lo! where this filent ftone
now weeps,*

The headstones of Sarah and Caleb Gould.

62

A Friend, a Wife, a Mother sleeps:
A heart within whose sacred cell
The peaceful Virtues lov'd to dwell:
Affect And soft humanity
were there.

Caleb Gould became a lock-keeper at Hambledon in 1777. He was a well known local figure who dressed in a long coat with many buttons and took a walk up the valley every day marking the spot that he reached by digging a cross in the ground – these were always known as 'Calebs Crosses'.

He apparently made bread in a large oven behind his cottage, and he sold this to bargemen and anyone else who wanted to buy it. It was said that he consumed a plate of onion porridge every night for his supper.

To the Memory of
CALEB GOULD
Who Died May 30,1836
Aged 92 Years
This world's a jest
And all things show it,
I thought so once,
But now I know it.

The simplest of epitaphs is that of John and Sarah Gillham. Sarah died many years after her husband, but it would seem that they were both very much loved and loving.

SACRED
to the Memory of
JOHN GILLHAM
WHO DIED AUGUST 3rd 1844
AGED 72 YEARS

The Gillham grave in the pretty churchyard of St Denys.

Also of
SARAH, HIS WIFE
WHO DIED OCTOBER 25th 1868
AGED 95 YEARS
Their end was peace
A husband kind, A Mother dear,
Two loving parents, sleepeth here.

These graves are in the pretty churchyard at St Denys, Stanford Dingley, and well worth a visit.

A husband and wife who, from their epitaph, appeared to have brought joy not only to each other but to many other people as well, were Henry and Alwine Brougham. Their gravestone in St John the Baptist, Crowthorne, is formal, but interesting.

In Loving Memory of
HENRY

WILLIAM
BROUGHAM
1854-1908
AND HIS WIFE
ALWINE
ROSA
BROUGHAM
1860-1927
THEY HAVE ACHIEVED SUCCESS
WHO HAVE LIVED UPRIGHTLY,
LAUGHED OFTEN AND LOVED MUCH.
WHO HAVE ALWAYS LOOKED FOR
THE GOOD IN OTHERS, AND GIVEN
THE BEST THEY HAD LEAVING THE
WORLD A LITTLE BETTER THAN
THEY FOUND IT.

There are three special examples of gravestones erected by loving husbands for their wives and that of Ellen Smallbone is one of them. It is to be found in St James's churchyard, Finchampstead, sheltering under a large rhodendron.

IN AFFECTIONATE REMEMBRANCE OF
ELLEN THE BELOVED WIFE OF
THOMAS SMALLBONE
WHO DEPARTED THIS LIFE
AUG 16.1900
AGED 70 YEARS
BE YE ALSO READY,
FOR IN SUCH AN HOUR
AS HE THINK NOT THE
SON OF MAN COMETH.

William Badcock and his children placed a gravestone for Mary, William's wife, in the churchyard of St John the Baptist, Crowthorne when she died in 1895. When Walter died in 1909, his name was added at the bottom. The gravestone is situated close to a path leading around the back of the church.

JESU MERCY
To the ever dear Memory
of
MARY HARRIET BADCOCK
who fell asleep
FEBRUARY 26TH 1895
A LOVING TRIBUTE
OF DEEP AFFECTION
FROM HER HUSBAND AND CHILDREN

Mary and William Badcock.

Film actress Diana Dors and her husband Alan Lake lie here.

R.I.P.

THY

WOUNDS, MY CURE, MY MORE

THAN TRUST ART THOU,

HADST THOU

NOT BORNE THEM

WHERE HAD I BEEN NOW?

ALSO OF

WILLIAM SALTER

BADCOCK

who died May 13th 1909.

AGED 77 YEARS.

The third simple, yet moving, epitaph from a husband to his wife is Emily Sampson's headstone which has a lovely blue and white cross motif near the top of it. It is located in St Mary's churchyard, East Shefford and reads:

EMILY JANE

THE BELOVED WIFE OF

WILLIAM SAMPSON

AND ELDEST DAUGHTER OF

EDWIN AND MARY ANN ROLFE,

WHO DIED JAN 6TH 1903

AGED 31 YEARS.

HER LAST WORDS WERE

LEAVE ME ALONE WITH JESUS.

Sometimes the tragedy of death is too much to bear for the remaining partner and so it was for Alan Lake, husband of the actress Diana Dors. Diana, who appeared in films, the theatre and on television, died of cancer at the age of fifty two, in 1984. Her death was widely and genuinely mourned. Her husband never got over his grief and he killed himself on October 10, 1984, the sixteenth anniversary of their meeting. They are buried side by side in Sunningdale Cemetery.

LOVE'S LAST GIFT
REMEMBRANCE
ALAN LAKE
1940-1984
TOGETHER FOREVER
only a whisper away.

ALWAYS
REMEMBERED
DIANA DORS
LAKE
1931 - 1984
FOREVER LOVED
Only a whisper away.

In St Gregory's churchyard, Welford, lie a husband and wife who were each famous in their own right – Howard Marshall and Jasmine Bligh. Howard was born on August 22,1900. He was a special correspondent on the *Westminster Gazette, Daily Telegraph* and *Daily Mail* and was an assistant news editor for the BBC in 1928.

In 1930 he was BBC Radio sports and special events commentator, becoming a war correspondent in the years 1943-45. Howard wrote many books, including *With Scott to the Pole; Rugger; Fiery Grains; Under Big Ben* and *Over to Tunis.*

He was co-founder of *The Angling Times, and Trout and Salmon.*

Howard was married to BBC's first woman television announcer, Jasmine Bligh, and he died on October 27, 1973.

HOWARD MARSHALL
BROADCASTER, AUTHOR
AND FISHERMAN
1900-1973
HE WAS MUCH LOVED

Jasmine Bligh, born in 1913, was descended from Captain Bligh of the *Bounty* and was cousin to the ninth Earl of Darnley. She became BBC Television's first female announcer on November 2, 1936. Twice divorced, she married Howard Marshall, and when he became ill during the late sixties and money was short, she bought a scarlet van and set up Bargain, a travelling second-hand clothes business. Certainly a very enterprising lady. Her last years, after suffering a stroke, were spent at Denville House, Northwood, a home

Journalist and broadcaster Howard Marshall lies here.

provided by the Actor's Charitable Trust, where she died in July, 1991.

Her headstone reads:

The headstone of Jasmine Bligh, Britain's first television announcer.

JASMINE BLIGH
21 MAY 1913
21JULY1991
First Television Announcer
Darling Mother
and Grandmother
Loved by all.

Other epitaphs to husbands and wives

Inside the church of St Michael the Archangel, Warfield, is a Latin inscription which says:

'*JOHN AND MARY VACHELL, scions of the ancient families of Vachell and Vincent, lie under this sacred marble. While they lived together they were living apart, and death itself has neither joined them together or separated them. They were both of them Catholics, she of the Anglican, he of the Roman faith. Both, nevertheless, lived temporately, piously, virtuously; and, which is a riddle, were friends with one another. They fell asleep in the Lord peacefully, the husband's age was 77, the wife's, 68. She on the 16th September, he on 8th November, A.D., 1640.*'

An undated epitaph for William Westall, who sang in the church choir for sixty six years, reads:

He went from the choir below
to the choir above.
Faringdon Parish church

To the Memory of
ELIZABETH
Wife of GEORGE DAY
who died May 24, 1880
Aged 33 Years
Of all the lines on tombstones found
Remember these be sure
Sin gives the conscience
such a wound
As none but Christ can cure.
St Mary, Cholsey

NOTABLE PEOPLE

I T IS not difficult to discover a great many graves for notable people in Berkshire's churchyards, although it could be said that every single grave and epitaph is notable for one reason or another.

The graves of the Booth family are to be found in the churchyard of St James in Finchampstead.

Here are Bramwell Booth, son of William and Catherine Booth, founders of the Salvation Army. Beside him lie his daughters, Dora and Olive, who both lived well into their nineties, and Catherine Bramwell-Booth, who lived to be 105 (see also Centenarians).

The Salvation Army was decribed in 1877 as 'a Salvation Army to carry the Blood of Christ and the Fire of the Holy Ghost to every corner of the world'. After years of Christian mission work the organisation took shape under the guiding hands of William and Catherine Booth. Military terms crept into the vocabulary of the mission. They were called the Hallelujah Army fighting the Devil, and William Booth was the General and Bramwell his Chief of Staff.

The mission became the Salvation Army in 1878, and a full uniform was adopted. The Army's newspaper *The War Cry* was launched the fol-lowing year and is still sold today.

Bramwell Booth succeeded his father as General in 1912. He was able to see the growth of the Salvation Armys' work during the First World War, offering comfort and sustenance to the troops in the trenches. He confounded those critics who claimed the Army would not survive once William Booth and his wife had died.

Bramwells' final illness brought periods of depression and sleeplessness. He was attacked by neuritis and his right arm became seriously affected. He died in December, 1984, aged ninety five.

Thomas Holloway was very well known in the middle of the nineteenth century and was a man of extraordinary abilities. Born on September 22, 1800, he spent the first twenty eight years of his life in the West Country before moving to London to seek better prospects. Soon after arriving he met Jane Driver whom he married and who enhusiastically supported her husband's ventures throughout their life together.

In 1836 Thomas Holloway became a merchant and foreign commercial agent and by helping one of his clients prepare an ointment from a secret recipe which was accepted for use at St Thomas's Hospital, managed to launch himself on the road to success.

The impressive tomb of Thomas Holloway and his wife Jane.

He prepared a harmless concoction known as Holloway's Family Ointment and once this was accepted by the Middlesex Hospital, Thomas built up a thriving business, believing that advertising was the key to his success.

In 1867 the couple, who had no children, bought Tittenhurst at Sunninghill, which later became famous as the home for two of the Beatles – first John Lennon and later, after his death, Ringo Starr.

Jane Holloway died in 1875 at the age of seventy one. Thomas, looking for new ways to spend his fortune, built a new hospital for the mentally afflicted at Virginia Water (opened by the Prince and Princess of Wales in 1885). He then came up with the idea of building a ladies' college in memory of his wife.

He bought ninety acres of land at Mount Lee, Egham Hill, on May 8, 1876, for what was to become The Royal Holloway College. Thomas had a bungalow built in the grounds so that he could watch the main building grow – a massive structure consisting of 1,000 rooms, with a chapel, library and an art gallery. The college was embellished with ornately designed scrolls, fruit, flowers and shells on every corner and pinnacle and over every door and window.

Thomas died shortly before the work was finished, having spent more than £400,000 on the land, buildings, furnishings and pictures. He left a further £300,000 to complete and endow the college.

It remained a women's college for nearly eighty years, before admitting male undergraduates in 1965. It has now merged with Bedford College, University of London and has places for nearly 3,000 undergraduates in the arts, sciences, and music.

Thomas Holloway died at his home in December 1883 and was buried beside his wife in the churchyard of St Michaels, Sunninghill. When Thomas died he was spending £50,000 a year on advertisements for his products and they had acquired a world wide reputation.

The arts are represented in Berkshire by two important epitaphs – one at Cookham and the other at Hurley.

In the churchyard of Holy Trinity, Cookham, stands the simple square gravestone of Stanley Spencer who died in December, 1959. It has been said that Stanley Spencer was the greatest English painter of the century. Born on June 30, 1891, he was given the nickname Cookham when he became a student at The Slade School in London. Stanley spent most of his life in Cookham which shaped his work throughout his career, and formed the setting for numerous biblical and figure paintings, as well as landscapes. Many Cookham scenes are recognisable

This stone marks the spot where Stanley Spencer's ashes are buried.

from his pictures. When his wife Hilda died in 1950 he expressed a wish to be buried beside her and arranged with her family for a double vault to be built in the Cookham Rise Cemetery close to Cliveden View.

However, after his death the executors decided that he should rest in the Cookham churchyard, not with Hilda. Stanley's body was cremated at Reading Crematorium in a private family ceremony. On the following day his ashes were taken to Cookham Church and laid to the left of the path which leads through the churchyard.

The Stanley Spencer Gallery in Cookham occupies the Victorian Methodist Chapel where Spencer was taken to worship as a child. It contains a permanent collection of his

Sir Kenneth Barnes.

work, together with letters, documents, memorabilia, and the pram in which Spencer wheeled his equipment when painting landscapes.

A great supporter of the arts is buried in St Mary the Virgin churchyard, Hurley. Sir Kenneth Ralph Barnes, born in 1878, became director of the Royal Academy of Dramatic Art in London, in 1909, and ensured that the academy prospered until his retirement in 1955. He never ceased to campaign for the training of young actors, which he regarded as essential to the well-being of the theatre.

He was greatly helped by his sisters, the actresses Irene and Violet Vanbrugh, and interest was shown in his work by Queen Elizabeth the Queen Mother, who in 1952 laid the foundation stone of the present Vanbrugh Theatre, built to replace the former students' theatre destroyed by bombing in 1941.

During the First World War Barnes served in India and Russia, and organised a concert party which toured Mesopotamia. He met and married Daphne Graham, a former student, in 1925. She had acted under the name of Mary Sheridan, and was a descendant of the playwright.

Kenneth Barnes was knighted in 1938 for his services to the stage.

A plain and simple headstone marks the grave of Sir Michael Hordern, a great British actor who died in 1986. He was born in Berkhampstead in 1914, was knight-

The stone marking the grave of Sir Michael Hordern and Lady Eve Hordern.

Here lies actress Mary Robinson.

ed in 1983 and died three years later. The grave is in St James's churchyard, Winterbourne.

In the churchyard of St Peter and St Andrew, Old Windsor, stands the impressive tomb of Mary Robinson, a well-known actress in the eighteenth century. She was most notable for her Shakespearean roles at Drury Lane, and at the height of her fame she was painted by Gainsborough, Reynolds and Romney.

Mary became the mistress of The Prince of Wales, later to become George IV, and she was admired not only by the famous artists of the day but also by Mary Wollstonecroft, William Godwin and David Garrick. The Duchess of Devonshire became her patron and Mary published many novels, plays and poetry.

She died in 1800, aged forty three, in poverty, while living at Englefield Cottage in Surrey. Her last wish was that she be buried in Old Windsor churchyard.

In 1952, Mary Robinson's great, great niece restored her tomb and it now stands with all its detailed inscription made much easier to read; most of it Mary wrote herself before she died:

Of Beauty's Isle, her daughter must declare, She who sleeps here was fairest of the fair. But ah! while Nature on her favourite smil'd and Genius claim'd his share in Beauty's child: Ev'n as they wove a garland for her brow Sorrow prepar'd a willowy wreath of woe Mix'd luried nightshade with the buds of May and twin'd her darkest cypress with the bay; In mildew tears steep'd every opening flow'r, Prey'd on the sweets, and gave the canker pow'r:

Yet, O may Pity's angel, from the grave This early victim of misfortune save! And as she springs to everlasting morn, May Glory's fadeless crown her soul adorn!"

On the other side of the tomb is a poem written by Mary Robinson:

O THOU! whose cold and senseless heart Ne'er knew affection's struggling sigh, Pass on, nor vaunt the stoic's art, Nor mock this grave with tearless eye. For oft when evening's purple glow Shall slowly fade from yonder steep, Fast o'er this sod the tear shall flow from eyes that only wake to weep. No wealth had she, nor power to sway; Yet rich in worth, and learning's store: She wept her sum-

*Large and flashy, the grave
of showman Billy Smart.*

mer hours away, She heard the win-
try storm no more. Yet o'er this low
and silent spot, Full many a bud of
Spring shall wave, While she, by all,
save ONE forgot, SHALL SNATCH A
WREATH BEYOND THE GRAVE!

William George (Billy) Smart
came from a fairground background
and in 1946 he staked all his
resources on a circus which appeared
regularly on television and travelled
all around the country.

He was a great showman, and once
rode an elephant through the streets
of Mayfair, parking it at a meter
before inserting a shilling.

Billy Smart collapsed and died on
September 25 1966, while conduct-
ing the band at his circus zoo at
Ipswich. His grave, large and showy,
like the man himself, is to be found
in St Peter's churchyard, Cranbourne:

BILLY SMART
DIED 25TH SEPTEMBER 1966

AND HIS LOVING WIFE
NELLIE SMART
DIED 16TH OCTOBER 1977
TOO DEARLY LOVED
TO BE FORGOTTEN.

Sir Charles Murray has a
sculpture in his memory
inside St Peter and St
Andrew, Old Windsor. He
was responsible for bringing
the first hippopotumus to
London Zoo. He secured this
animal while acting as
Consul in Egypt. It arrived in
1850 and lived on at the zoo
for nearly thirty years.

Sir Charles spent his last years at
Old Windsor, although he died
abroad in 1895, aged eighty nine. As
a diplomat he was sent to the Court
of Persia, and it was chiefly due to
the false charges made against him
by the Shah's unscrupulous Grand
Vizier, that England declared War on
Persia in 1856.

In America, when a young man, he
fell in love with a woman whose
father forbade him ever to see her. It
was not until the father died fourteen
years later that they were married.

In All Saints, Binfield, is an epi-
taph to another famous diplomat, Sir
Donald Macnabb, who died on
January 30, 1913, aged seventy nine.

For many years he was Deputy
Commissioner and subsequently
Commissioner of Peshawur in the
Punjab. His epitaph records:

BORN JANUARY 5TH, 1833.
DIED JANUARY 30TH, 1913.
Blessed are the dead which die in the Lord, they rest from their labours and their Works do follow them.

Charles Hill had been a diplomat for twenty seven years, serving Queen Victoria as one of her own Messengers, when he died suddenly at The Home Office, London, in 1869. He is buried in St Andrew's churchyard, Clewer, sharing the same impressive monument with his wife Mary Ann Hill who died nineteen years after her husband in 1888.

Mary Ann was Nanny to all the princes and princesses from 1841 to 1859. The children's names are carved around the gravestone slab for it was they who paid for the stone.

When she retired Queen Victoria gave Mary a bath chair, with a white pony called Dukey to pull it. The pony had its own stable built at the bottom of Mary's garden and in front of it a greenhouse, both commanded by the Queen, in which a cutting from the Hampton Court vine was planted.

Mary was allowed to visit any part of Windsor Castle whenever she chose, and Queen Victoria would often ride out and visit her for tea.

During Mary's final illness the Queen and other members of the royal family were frequent visitors, and there were many royal wreaths at her funeral, as there had been for her

Charles and Mary Hill, the diplomat and the royal nanny.

husband, Charles.

In All Saints churchyard, Sutton Courtenay, is the tomb of Prime Minister Herbert Henry Asquith.

The son of a manufacturer, he was born in 1852 and when his father died, was sent to the City of London School where he became head ,and spent much of his time listening to public speeches and debates. After

The tomb of Prime Minister Herbert Asquith.

obtaining a scholarship to Balliol and receiving academic distinction, he was called to the Bar.

Herbert Asquith married while still young and aged thirty four entered Parliament for East Fife, six years later joining Gladstone's government as Home Secretary. In 1905 he joined Campbell-Bannerman's Liberal Ministry as Chancellor of the Exchequer introducing an avalanche of social reforms, including pensions and unemployment insurance.

After Britain entered the First World War he headed the Coalition Government for eighteen months until he was ousted in December, 1916, lacking, according to Lloyd George, 'that vision, imagination and initiative' essential to every War Minister.

Asquith resigned leadership of the Liberal Party in 1926 and spent his final years living by the river in a conversion of three houses, which he called The Wharf.

He died after a series of strokes in 1928, and at his own request received no public funeral.

A rather overwhelming, but impressive tombstone in the church-yard of St Peter and St Andrew, Old Windsor, is in memory of Esther Jane, widow of Richard Brinsley Sheridan, the eighteenth century playwright, who allowed his parliamentary and social ambitions to take precedence over his writing.

Sheridan had eloped to France with his first wife, Elizabeth Linley, having fought two duels with her other admirers. It was she who had warned him that he would do best to consider politics as an amusement

Sheriden's widow Esther Jane is buried here.

and to look elsewhere for wealth and independence. He did not take her advice and Elizabeth died whilst still quite young.

He then married Esther Jane, daughter of Newton Ogle, Dean of Winchester, who also had no control over her husband. It must have been most tragic for her during her long illness to have known that Sheridan was lying in a room next to hers living in desperate squalor, wrecked by drink and discarded by friends who had decided he was beyond their help.

He died in the summer of 1816. Esther died in October 27, 1817.

SACRED TO THE MEMORY OF
ESTHER JANE,
DAUGHTER OF NEWTON OGLE D.D.
DEAN OF WINCHESTER
OF KIRKLEY IN NORTHUMBERLAND
AND WIDOW OF THE RIGHT HONOURABLE
RICHARD BRINSLEY SHERIDAN,
AFTER ENDURING WITH UNEXAMPLED
RESIGNATION AND HEROISM
AN ILLNES PROTRACTED
DURING FIVE YEARS
AND AGGRAVATED BY EVERY SPECIES OF
PAIN AND SELF DENIAL,
SHE WAS RELEASED ON THE 27TH DAY OF
OCTOBER, 1817, AGED 41 YEARS.
ADMIRED IN SOCIETY AND ADORED IN
DOMESTIC LIFE, IT WAS RESERVED FOR
THE MORE TRYING HOURS OF SOLITUDE
AND SUFFERING TO CALL FORTH THE
ENERGIES OF A MIND IN WHICH THE
UTMOST FEMININE SENSIBILITY
WAS SUPPORTED BY A MORE THAN MANY
FORTITUDE. THIS STONE IS ERECTED

*AS A FEEBLE TRIBUTE OF REGRET AND
GRATITUDE BY AN ONLY SON
THE OBJECT OF HER ARDENT AND
UNVARYING LOVE OF UNROUNDED AND
INVALUABLE BENEFITS AND WHO IN LOS-
ING THE BEST OF PARENTS, THE DEAREST
OF FRIENDS, THE MOST DELIGHTFUL OF
COMPANIONS, WAS SUSTAINED BY THE
HUMBLE HOPE THAT HER LENGTHENED
TRIALS HAD AT LENGTH OBTAINED A
LASTING RECOMPENSE.*

Thomas Thellusson Carter is one example of the many religious men and women who have devoted their lives to God and to caring for the people of Berkshire.

Born at Eton in 1808, he lived

**The 'saint' of Clewer,
Thomas Thellusson Carter.**

under five reigning monarchs until the grand age of ninety three, serving as Rector for Clewer for fifty seven years.

Thomas Carter was the founder and warden of the Sisterhood of St John the Baptist (see Miscellaneous) and in the parish of Clewer was revered as a saint. Even today a Mass of Thanksgiving is said every October 29, which is observed locally as 'his' day.

The epitaph in St Andrews churchyard, Clewer, records details of both Thomas Carter and his wife Mary Anne:

*HERE RESTS IN CHRIST
THOMAS THELLUSSON
CARTER
RECTOR OF THIS PARISH
1844-1880
FOUNDER & WARDEN
OF THE SISTERHOOD
OF ST JOHN THE BAPTIST
BORN MARCH 19.1808
DEPARTED
OCT 28.1901
GRANT THEM O LORD
ETERNAL REST.*

In the same churchyard is the simple stone cross memorial of Mariquita Tennant who was the Spanish widow of an English clergyman. Windsor was a garrison town and beer houses and brothels were commonplace.

In 1860 there were seven beer houses and four houses of ill repute

All that remains of Marquita Tennant's grave.

in Clewer Lane alone. The brothels provided the only means of earning a living for some uneducated girls from poor families. Mrs Tennant provided shelter for some of these girls at a house called The Limes near Clewer Church.

If a girl stayed rescued, she was required to change her surname to Magdalen after the woman who was a sinner in the Gospels. In the churchyard at Clewer there are many white stone crosses with the name Magdalen on them and nothing else.

There was a mystery regarding Mariquita Tennant's grave. She died in 1856 and her coffin, full sized and marble with the lid bursting open, revealed where the body should lie. A Bible and cross lay in the vacant place upon the grave clothes, and on the inside of the half raised lid were the words *Non Est Hic, Sed Resurrexit* (Not Here, But Risen).

No one knows what happened to this rather grotesque coffin, but the stone cross that now marks Mariquita Tennant's grave, even though the epitaph is mostly below ground level, is a fitting tribute to a remarkable woman.

There is another interesting monument at St Michael, Letcombe Bassett.

Shaded by a large yew tree the epitaph remembers a Maori chief, called George King Hipango, who died in England in 1871. Hori King Hipango was the son of an influential chief of Wancanui. His father had visited England in 1855, accompanied by the Rev Richard Taylor, to convey gifts to Queen Victoria and Prince Albert.

A Maori chief's grave at Letcombe Bassett.

Job Lousley's impressive memorial.

Hori (George) Hipango died, aged only nineteen, whilst also visiting England with Mr Taylor. There is no record of why he died so young and why he was buried at Letcombe Bassett.

Berkshire has its share of unusual memorials, but none come much stranger than that belonging Job Lousley, who is buried at the back of St Mary's Church, Hampstead Norreys.

Job came from an old Hampstead family and apart from being well known for his work on the county council, which he served as a alder-

man for eleven years, he was also a well-loved Lord of the Manor.

His father had been a farmer, and following in his footsteps, Job started with one wagon and ended up with four farms. He specialised in shire horse breeding and won many prizes at local and national shows.

He died in 1855 and had expressed a wish to be buried on his own land in Beech Wood, but the Bishop of Oxford refused permission to use this site and he was, instead, buried in a part of the churchyard that had once belonged to him (When the church-yard had been extended some of Job

Lousley's fields were used).

The wives of his tenant farmers and farmworkers gathered together broken ploughshares and other farm implements. Two cartloads were sent to Bucklebury Foundry where they were melted down and used to create a cast iron monument. It rises tier by tier, like a huge wedding cake, and is surmounted by an obelisk.

Names of the Lousley family have been added throughout the years, the last being that of Conrad Offa Lousley, who died in 1962. He was the ninth child of Luke, eldest son of Job Lousley. It is a nice touch to know that because of his father's wishes, Luke placed a granite memorial on the place in Beech Wood where his father used to gaze over the manorial lands.

Berkshire has had its fair share of artists to be proud of and certainly the name of Edward Polehampton is still revered today in Twyford, although very little of his work remains. Although he painted some portraits, a great deal of his work centred on panels of allegorical and heraldic design which were often used on the magnificent coaches in the late 1600s and early 1700s.

The story of Polehampton's early life is still largely unknown and based only on stories circulated since 1666. It was said that the landlord of the Rose and Crown Inn, Twyford, found Polehampton on his doorstep on Christmas Eve, 1666. He was destitute and alone and the landlord cared for him until he was well enough to set out on the road to London to seek his fortune.

Polehampton became a pupil of a London painter Henry Lyne, and was admitted to the Painter Stainers Company, remaining an honorary member until his death.

Apart from his own work he took pupils of his own and was also a print seller. As he prospered he was able to buy property and thus added to his wealth.

Edward Polehampton died in 1722 and according to his wishes was buried in the churchyard at St Nicholas, Hurst, but it was Twyford that benefited from his generosity during his lifetime and from the instructions left in his will. Opposite the Rose and Crown Inn, where supposedly the landlord had been so kind to him, Polehampton ordered the foundations to be laid for a school chapel, a master's house, and a charity to benefit poor boys of the village.

In his will it was stated that the school should house ten poor boys between the ages of eight and fifteen. No pupil could remain after that age as his place must be taken by another child. Each boy would receive £10 a year for clothing. A master was to be appointed, earning £40 a year, and if possible the master should also be a minister who could officiate at the chapel where a service should be held every Sunday morning and afternoon.

Although the chapel was never consecrated it was in use until the present church was built in Twyford in 1846.

In 1888 a new state school was built bearing the name Polehampton, although part of the charity school building still remains opposite a private house which was once the Rose and Crown Inn.

Another famous Victorian artist is buried in Holy Trinity churchyard, Cookham. Fred Walker lived for only thirty five years, yet he had built up a considerable reputation for such a short life. Born in London in 1840, he came from an artistic family and when young was apprenticed to a wood engraver. He became known for his work in periodicals such as *The Cornhill Magazine.* Through this met Thackeray whose *Adventures of Philip* he illustrated.

Walker was also an ardent fisherman. He would sit at work in a punt moored by Monkey Island, using as a palette a small piece of varnished wood – usually the punt's backboard – and would stop from time to time to cast over the nose of a large trout, which he rarely managed to catch.

Fred Walker, a very popular figure in Cookham, died in 1875. There was genuine grief and sadness when his body was laid to rest in Cookham churchyard. Later a plaque bearing his portrait in profile was erected in at the back of Holy Trinity Church and part of the inscription reads:

This is the painter of 'The Harbour of Refuge' and 'The Vagrants' and he is believed to have been the original of Little Billie in George Du Maurier's 'Trilbys'.

Other epitaphs to notable people

*Sacred To the Memory of
William Mackinnon Efq
who departed this Life
on the 7th Day of February
in the Year of our
Lord 1809
Aged 75 Years
He was Defcended from an ancient
Familyin the Weftern Iflands of
Scotlandand born in the Ifland of
Antiguain which during many Years
he held a feat in his Majeftys Council
He was pofsefsed of a mofft amiable
Difpofition and remarkable for the
purity of his Morals and the
B enevolence and Integrity of his
Heart.*
All Saints, Binfield

TRADES AND PROFESSIONS

MANY churchyards in Berkshire bear testimony to men and women who were proud of their trades and professions, and wished to be remembered by future generations. Here are shepherds, farmers and blacksmiths; surgeons, doctors and vicars; engineers, architects and many others whose epitaphs mention an occupation. In some cases the carving of implements shows the trade or profession.

The inauguration of the fast mail coach service between Bristol and London, in 1784, introduced a vibrancy to daily life through its speed and time-keeping. As travelling became easier, more people visited towns and these improved their amenities to cope with the extra influx. Towns were still mainly marketing centres and because of their industries of brewing, malting and milling, were dependent on agricultural produce, therefore maintaining traditional links with the countryside.

Towns provided banking and legal services, but most of their clients lived in the country. The products of local farms and local craftsmen were bought and sold, thus again making town and country dependent on each other.

Throughout the nineteenth century the improvement of transport facilities, together with the efficiency of postal services drew towns and villages even closer together – the village shops were able to use more of the worlds' products and enlarge their stock.

Sometimes it was necessary for the people in less prosperous parts of the county to have multiple occupations – for example, at East Ilsley, Joseph Badcock was draper, mercer, grocer, chemist and agent for Guinness stout.

Most villages, or towns for that matter, probably considered their vicars to hold a most important profession, and for them to act accordingly. In the eighteenth century the Vicar of Beenham was the Rev Thomas Stackhouse (buried at St Mary's, Beenham), author of *The History of the Bible*. It is difficult to imagine what his parishioners must have thought of him as he performed the task of writing mainly at Jack's Booth, a public house on the Bath Road. Saturday nights writing and drinking were followed by Sunday sermons on the sin of drunkeness.

In St Mary's Church, Longcott, is a memorial to Ernest Carter and his wife Lilian. She was the daughter of Tom Hughes who wrote *Tom Brown's Schooldays*, and when she married Ernest he was a schoolmaster. He was ordained shortly afterwards and was soon working in London's East End as Vicar of Whitechapel. A great

Schoolmaster Henry Marshall lies here.

A memorial to a man who remained a teacher all his life is to be found in St Mary's churchyard, Wargrave. The epitaph, for Henry Marshall who was Master of the Piggott School for thirteen years, was erected by the trustees of the school, who must have had great respect for Marshall as a teacher:

> HENRY MARSHALL
> BORN SEP. 5. 1840,
> ENTERED INTO REST
> NOV. 13. 1883,
> UNTIL THE DAY DAWN,
> AND THE SHADOWS FLEE AWAY

Members of the medical profession can be found in most churchyards around Berkshire. Perhaps a slightly different epitaph is that of George Halpin, whose simple inscription can be found on the wrought iron gate leading up to All Saints Parish Church, Swallowfield.

> IN MEMORY OF GEORGE HALPIN
> DOCTOR & FRIEND 1882-1958

many of the population in their parish were Jewish so the Carters first learnt Yiddish and then taught it to others.

After fourteen years of continuous hard work, often close to hardship and poverty, they were in such need of a rest that they booked a second-class passage to America in 1912. The name of the ship they sailed on was *Titanic.*

It was revealed, once the ship had sunk, that Lilian had been offered a place in one of the lifeboats, but had refused to leave her husband. Thus two hours or so later they became two more victims among the 1,500 passengers who went down with the huge liner.

George Halpin's memorial gates.

Another epitaph for a doctor can be found in Holy Trinity churchyard, Bracknell for Thomas Croft, who died in 1906 and is buried with his wife Eliza. He was listed as Public Vaccinator, Registrar of Births and Deaths, Factory Surgeon, and also Poor Law Medical officer, for which he received the sum of £40 a year, later raised to £50.

Surgeon Henry Poole Palmer died aged only twenty six. His memorial can be seen in St Giles, Reading. Apparently he died at his home in Church Street, Reading, after a few days' illness, and his epitaph with only a few words missing here and there, is a moving one:

> He came . . . and was cut
> down like a flower
> To the Memory of
> Henry Poole Palmer
> Surgeon of this town
> who died on the 6th Nov.1839
> at the early age of 26
> having fallen a victim to the
> typhus fever caught in the
> zealous discharge of his
> professional duties
> as medical officer to the Reading
> Union
> by his death the poor . . .
> been deprived of a fri . . .
> whose skill and kindness . . .
> be long and deeply lamen . . .

James Breach, also a surgeon, died aged seventy five on December 10, 1903. His gravestone is slightly diffi-cult to read with lichen creeping across the inscription, and stands in the churchyard of St Clements, Ashampstead:

> *In*
> *Loving Memory*
> *of*
> JAMES BREACH OF YATTENDON
> SURGEON
> BORN AUGUST 24th 1828
> DIED DECEMBER 10th 1903 ALSO OF
> ELIZABETH MARY,
> HIS WIFE
> DIED JANUARY 14th 1913.

George Henry Watts.

Yet another surgeon buried in Berkshire is George Henry Watts whose memorial stands like a white ghost in a tangled undergrowth of willow and creeping ivy in St Mary's churchyard, Bucklebury.

He lived in Thatcham and died aged fifty one in 1879. His grave is shared by his wife Sarah, who lived on until she was eighty three.

Sir Morell Mackenzie was a distinguished throat specialist and first rose to prominence in his field by introducing the laryngoscopic mirror to Britain. He wrote many research papers and books on diseases of the throat and in 1883 founded the first hospital in the world, at Golden Square, London, to specialise in diseases of the throat.

Between 1887 and 1888 he was involved in major controversy concerning Crown Prince Frederick of Prussia, who had complained of a sore throat. Sir Morell disagreed with the German doctors who had been about to operate, believing the Prince to be suffering from cancer of the larynx, and instead prescribed only minor surgery and a rest cure.

For this precription Mackenzie was showered with money and decorations. However, thirteen months later Frederick died of cancer of the larynx. Germany levelled vituperation at him and in 1888 Mackenzie wrote a book called *The Fatal Illness of the Noble Frederick* which sold more than 100,000 copies in a fortnight and contained abuse and accusations aimed at the professors of the University of Berlin.

In June 1888 the Council of The Royal College of Surgeons condemned his book and he was forced to resign his membership of The Royal College of Physicians. He died in London, aged fifty five on February 3, 1892, and is buried close

Disgraced throat specialist Sir Morell Mackenzie lies here.

to the main path leading to St Mary's Parish Church, Wargrave.

SIR MORELL MACKENZIE, Kt.,
M.D.G.C.H.,
BORN JULY 7th 1837,
DIED FEB 3rd 1892.
LIVES OF GREAT MEN ALL REMIND US
WE CAN MAKE OUR LIVES SUBLIME
AND DEPARTING LEAVE BEHIND US
FOOTPRINTS ON THE SANDS OF TIME.

Just like doctors and surgeons, judges and men of the legal profession hold their clients' futures in their hands. Inside All Saints Church, Ascot, is a memorial, jewelled and enamelled, with a portrait of Sir John Huddleston in his robes as a judge.

Born in Dublin on September 8,

1815, and educated in Ireland, Huddleston matriculated at Trinity College, Dublin, entered Gray's Inn on April 118, 1836, and was called to the Bar three years later. At the Old Bailey and on circuit he acquired an extensive criminal practice.

He took silk in 1857, and was elected a Bencher of his Inn, of which he was treasurer, in 1859 and 1868. After unsuccessfully contesting several constituencies he was returned to Parliament for Canterbury, for the Conservatives, in 1865, and in the following year carried through the Hop Trade Bill which was a useful measure intended to prevent the employment of fraudulent marks in that industry.

Huddleston contested Norwich successfully in 1874 and was Judge Advocate of the Fleet from 1865 to 1875, when he was called to the degree of Sergeant-at-law, raised to the Bench of the Common Pleas, and knighted.

During the last ten years of his life he suffered from a chronic and painful disease, and some of the cases he tried severely damaged his health. He died at his town house in South Kensington in 1890.

John Clark's gravestone is not only difficult to read, but stands with its back to a very busy road merging with two other roads outside Datchet's parish churchyard.

Another man of the law, Clark was an attorney and a clerk of the Central Criminal Court who died on the August 5, 1858.

Many fine buildings in Britain owe much to the talent of Berkshire architects. Thomas Rickman was the son of a Maidenhead grocer and it is said that while he was still in his teens he painted 5,000 model figures of military uniforms, with great precision, and then arranged them in front of pictures of military buildings.

He became a famous church architect, and he competed for the commission to build the Houses of Parliament. After his death he left more than 2,000 drawings of Gothic architecture. Thomas Rickman is buried at All Saints Parish church, Maidenhead.

One of the most eminent Victorian architects is buried beside St Peter and St Paul Church, Yattendon. Alfred Waterhouse's working life covered the second half of the nineteenth century and spanned the building worlds of London and the provinces. He was born in 1830 to a family of Quakers. Waterhouse was president of the Royal Institute of British Architects for three years, and produced designs that were simultaneously modern while satisfying a patron's sense of history and permanence.

Waterhouse designed mansions, club houses, colleges, churches and town halls. By the early 1880s he

The grave of Victorian engineer Sir Daniel Gooch.

was indisputably the leading architect of the kingdom – the Prudential building in Holborn, Manchester Town Hall, the National Liberal Club and the National History Museum were all his creations.

In 1878 Waterhouse moved to Yattendon with his wife Bessie and five children, building a new house on the beacon hilltop near the village. He became a churchwarden and was responsible for many improvements to the local church, as well as improving the bus shelter!

Two noted engineers are buried in Berkshire – each famous in his own right. Sir Daniel Gooch was born in Northumberland in 1816 and started his engineering career making coffin handles. After serving a railway apprenticeship in the works of Robert Stephenson, he was only twenty one when appointed Locomotive Superintendent of the Great Eastern Railway on the recommendation of Isambard Kingdom Brunel. During the twenty seven years he held that

post, Gooch made remarkable engines capable of speeds never before thought possible, and also founded the railway works at Swindon. His genius and engineering knowledge played a considerable part in the development of the railways.

In 1864 Gooch resigned to inaugurate telegraphic communications between Britain and America, and two years later was successful in despatching the first cable message across the Atlantic, for which he received a baronetcy.

However, he was soon recalled by his former employers who had encountered great administrative difficulties after his departure. Once Gooch had become chairman of the board of directors, he quickly restored the railway to a sound condition.

He had a great deal to do with the building of the Severn Tunnel and was part owner of a steamship called *The Great Eastern* which unfortunately ended its days as a floating circus.

Daniel Goochs' first wife predeceased him by some years and it is said that she appeared to him in a dream telling him to marry Emily Burder, a friend of hers.

His first wife is buried with him, but the second wife is buried in a grave of her own, some yards away. Gooch died in 1889, and is buried in quite a large plot in St Andrew's churchyard, Clewer:

> SIR DANIEL GOOCH, BARONET
> OF CLEWER PARK, WINDSOR
> BORN 24th AUGUST 1816.
> DIED 15th OCTOBER 1889
> I KNOW THAT MY REDEEMER LIVETH

Inside the church of St James the Less, Pangbourne, is a plaque in memory of another engineer, Sir Benjamin Baker, designer of the Forth Rail Bridge.

Born on March 31, 1840, in Somerset, Baker attended grammar school at Cheltenham, and when he was sixteen was apprenticed at Neath Abbey Ironworks. In 1860 he left and became assistant to William Wilson, who designed Victoria Station. Two years later he joined the staff of Sir John Fowler and became involved in construction of the Metropolitan and District lines of the London Underground. This project required considerable ingenuity to overcome the many hazards caused by difficult soils, underground water and the ruins of Roman and other civilisa-

tions. He incorporated an ingenious energy conservation measure in the construction of the Central line by dipping the line between stations to reduce the need for both braking to a halt, and for the increase in power required to accelerate away.

It was with great reluctance that the government permitted an attempt to build a bridge across the Forth. Baker was put in charge. A site allowing the use of the little island of Inchgarvie was chosen as a foundation for the central pier, and the bridge was finally opened on the March 4, 1890, by the Prince of Wales. It has been in service ever since. For this achievement Baker was knighted by Queen Victoria.

Although it was the Forth Bridge that made Baker famous, he undertook many other projects, both in Britain and abroad, and one interesting piece of work was the design of a large wrought iron vessel in which Cleopatra's Needle, the obelisk on the Thames Embankment, was transported to England. The Needle was lost at sea, but when found at a later date, it was discovered that it had been safely preserved within the hull of Bakers' ship.

In his later years he built up a large practice and was held in great esteem as a successful engineer who respected the theory of engineering. Baker was made a Fellow of the Royal Society in 1880 and died a bachelor on May 19, 1907.

Maidenhead has two astronomers buried in St Andrews, the first being David Gregory. He died in 1708 and was a friend of Sir Isaac Newton, who helped him attain the Savilian Professorship of Astronomy at Oxford.

William Lassells, who was born in Lancashire is the second. He was a self-taught astronomer, who along with Sir William Herschel, became famous for his skill in making reflecting telescopes. Whilst others were unable to follow the movements of comets, Lassells could make important discoveries using his own twenty foot telescope. In the first year of using it he discovered a satellite on the newly discovered planet Neptune, and two years later discovered a satellite of Saturn and another of Uranus.

Lassells moved to Malta with a new instrument that had a four foot aperture and was able to catalogue 600 nebulae. He finally moved his observatory to Maidenhead where he died in 1880.

In St Laurence's Church, Upton, Slough, a stone tablet under the tower marks the memorial to Sir William Herschel who died in 1822.

Born in Germany in 1738, Herschel joined the Hanoverian Guards as an oboist and, in 1757, came to England, having deserted his regiment. He was granted a full pardon by George III.

At first he made his living by training the band of the Durham Militia, and thereafter moved to Doncaster where he taught music. The study of harmony eventually led to an interest in astronomy and inspired his resolution to take nothing on trust. Herschel's brother helped him buy a small reflector which enabled him to study the heavens in much more detail.

On March 13, 1781, whilst living in Bath, he discovered the planet Uranus and investigated the distribution of stars in the Milky Way, concluding that some of the nebulae he could see were separate star systems.

Later he moved to Slough and King George paid £4,500 for a giant telescope to be erected at the astronomer's home.

The framework formed a conspicuous object which for many years could be seen by anyone travelling between London and Oxford.

Herschel's epitaph reads:
Coelorum percipit claustra
which translates as
He broke through the barriers
of the heavens
an apt inscription for an astronomer

Buried in St John the Evangalist, Littlewick, is another astronomer – George Dunn. He was interested, too in arboriculture, horology and old books; his library was sold for £32,000 at Sotheby's after his death.

A sad story relates that Dunn suffered from a broken romance, for on the morning of his wedding day his bride-to-be ran away with his brother. The wedding breakfast, which had been set out ready, was left untouched for the rest of his life. George Dunn died in 1912, aged forty seven.

There are probably many farmers buried in Berkshire who wish they could have had an astronomer's insight when it came to managing their crops and animals.

However, Jethro Tull was perhaps the most remarkable of agricultural pioneers and his achievements in the progress of scientific farming have had a continuing effect on arable farming processes.

Jethro Tull's stone, Basildon

Born in Basildon in 1674 to an old established Berkshire family, Tull trained to become a lawyer and was called to the Bar at the age of twenty five. Ill-health obliged him to live in the country where he ran his farms at Howberry, near Wallingford, and at Basildon. He soon began to deplore the wastefulness of the traditional practice of heavy seeding, ordering his men to make channels into which smaller amounts of seed could be sown. But the men refused to obey him, disliking any changes in procedures.

Tull, therefore, set himself to design a mechanical drill to sow seed in rows, thus inventing the first agricultural machine with internal moving parts.

Eight years later, he moved to his farm near to Hungerford, calling it Prosperous. His need to go on improving the ways of farming led him to travel on the continent, studying plant growth and soil nutrients. He invented a horse-hoe, and wrote books about his inventions. Some of his theories proved unworkable, but a lot of his experimental work contributed to a great deal of improvement in farming practices, which in turn helped to better the crops. It also helped to keep farm animals alive through the winter, instead of slaughtering them and salting the meat.

Jethro Tull died in 1740, but the exact site of his grave is unknown. The stone in the churchyard of St Bartholomew, Lower Basildon, was put up by the late Gordon Beale in 1941. It reads:

To the Memory of
JETHRO TULL
Pioneer of Mechanised Agriculture
Author of Horte-Hoing Husbandry
Baptised in this Church
30th March 1674
Buried here 9th March 1740.
Man is a Glasse, Life is as Water,
weakely walled about
Sin brought in Death. Death
breaks the Glass
so runs the water out.
Requiescat in pace.

Even today farmers claim that their's is not an easy profession, but certainly in the eighteenth and nine-teenth centuries farmers and their labourers suffered a great deal from occupational illnesses, very often caused by the hard work they had to do, or from the effects of the weather conditions. Severe weather often ruined harvests and even if the harvest could be brought in safe and sound, the labourers' hours were shortened and wages reduced.

Sometimes this meant men could be out of work for three or four months, causing great poverty and hardship for their families. For the men who worked with cattle or sheep anthrax was often the cause of death,

Edward Smith's tombstone.

and rheumatism and arthritis killed many who worked outside and in the cold. Yet some farmers lived to a good age, as did Edward Smith, whose gravestone can be found in St Mary's churchyard, White Waltham – although it does appear from his epitaph that he lived a very careful life.

To the Memory
of
Mr EDWARD SMITH
upwards of fifty years farmer of
this Parish who through a Life of
temperence and fobriety departed
this Life July 14:1786,
In the 84 Year of his Age.
Alfo of
Mrs MARGARET SMITH

Wife of the
above
Mr EDWARD SMITH
who departed this life June 9:1781,
In the 76 Year of her Age.

Headstones for farmers showing agricultural implements are fairly common, but the gravestone for William Lyford is a splendid example considering its age. The design of plough, sickle, hay fork, reaping hook and rake is grouped around a central sheaf and the epitaph is still almost legible:

In Memory of
WILLIAM LYFORD who died
Jan: 9th: 1784, Aged 58.

The intricately worked
headstone for William Lyford.

With Patience to the laſt he did ſub-
mit And Murmur'd not at what the
Lord thought. After a lingering illneſs
Grief & Pain, When Doctors ſkill &
Phiſic prov'd in vain, He with a
Chriſtian Courage did Refign His
foul to God at his Appointed time.

This epitaph can be found under a large yew tree at the front of St Mary's church, Winkfield. The church itself was built in 1300, with the brick tower added in 1629.

Inside there are pillars straight down the middle of the aisle. They were built in Queen Elizabeth I's reign, but when the church was partly built, so the tale says, the Devil came and pulled it down. Eventually a pact was made with the Devil that he could build half the church, so the pillars were installed again, to divide the church between the Devil and the Lord. Many old Winkfield people would not be buried on the Devil's side, and even now when brides and grooms come down the aisle they have to part company to get round the pillars. They are an amazing and unusual sight in this lovely old church.

The uncertainties of the British weather must have affected many trades and professions in their day to day work, just as it does today. Certainly gardeners and nurserymen needed to adjust their lives to the seasons the same as the farmers had to.

In St Andrew's churchyard,

Bailiff Thomas Melrose.

Clewer, lies Thomas Melrose, an employee of Field Marshall Earl Harcourt. The dates of his birth and death are now illegible, but most of his epitaph can still be seen and is well worth reading.

To the Memory
of
Thomas Melrose,
Bailiff & Gardener
to
Field-Marshall Earl
Harcourt for
29 years
during which period
he was distinguished for his
intelligence, modesty and integrity

and esteemed by his master.

Market gardening has been carried out since the eighteenth century. Starting in a small way, it soon became possible after about 1838, to send large quantities of fresh vegetables, fruit and flowers by rail to London, as well as selling to the more prosperous towns such as Windsor. This attracted more gardeners to become nurserymen and market gardeners.

John Standish, whose memorial stands in a pretty secluded spot in the churchyard of All Saints, Ascot, was one of these nurserymen and was obviously respected both in his trade and personal life.

THIS MEMORIAL
IS ERECTED BY
A FEW PERSONAL FRIENDS
TO THE MEMORY OF
JOHN STANDISH
NURSERYMAN
BORN MARCH 25th 1814,
DIED JULY 24th 1875
ALSO LUCY HIS WIFE
WHO DIED AUGUST 13th 1884
AGED 79 YEARS
BLESSED ARE THE PURE IN HEART.

Shepherds deserve a special mention when it comes to epitaphs in Berkshire and none more so than the one for Charles Napper who is buried on the south side of St Peter and St Paul, Appleford:

The grave of John Standish at Ascot.

Born 1806. December 26
Died 1872.Aged 66 Years.
Died of a bad cold.

There were probably many shepherds who died from bad colds, but Charles Napper's epitaph seemed very much to the point!

Shepherds were usually highly regarded members of a rural community and very often their epitaphs would record that fact in one way or another. Over the centuries it was the custom that when a shepherd died, a piece of sheep's wool would be placed in his coffin as proof of his calling.

He could then convince St Peter that there was good reason for his irregular church attendance. At times his sheep needed him, even on the Sabbath, and as a good shepherd he could never neglect his flock!

An epitaph for Thomas Pope, a shepherd, is to be found in the churchyard of St Peter and St Andrew, Old Windsor, although it is mostly illegible, the epitaph records show just how highly this particular shepherd was regarded:

THOMAS POPE
SHEPHERD
(who died) July (the) 20th 18(32)
Aged 96 years
cheerfully laborious to an advanced age, he was much esteemed by all classes of his neighbours some of whom have paid this tribute of respect to the memory of a faithful, industrious, and contented peasant.
Also Phoebe, wife of the above who died March 2nd 1843 aged 90 years.

Thomas Brent, who lived and worked in Hurst, was obviously proud of his craftsmanship as a blacksmith, to the extent that he made his own wrought iron headstone. He died, aged eighty, on September 11, 1885.

Brent's apprentice added the date when Thomas died. Usually, blacksmiths have long and detailed epitaphs that list the tools with which they plied their trade, but Thomas Brent went one better and hung a hammer, pliers, axe and mallet from

each end of his headstone.

In a way it is a shame that such a striking headstone should be hidden away at the back of St Nicholas churchyard, Hurst, fighting for space between a wheelbarrow, a small trailer and a large pile of rubbish.

Carpenters very often had headstones that showed the tools of their trade, but the tombstone for Thomas Philips is a very grand affair, surrounded with iron railings and in quite good repair. It stands beside the path leading to the church of St

Left: Blacksmith Thomas Brent's unusual iron grave marker.

Below: A grand grave for carpenter Thomas Philips.

Andrew in East Hagbourne and the epitaph is well worth reading.

Here lyeth the body of Thomas
Philips, son of
Matthew Philips, of this parifh whofe
known skills and diligence in his pro-
feffion joined with great Probity in
his Dealings gained him that
Reputation in bufinefs which recom-
mended him to be carpenter to their
Majefty's King George the firft and
King George the second.
He Dyed the 14 day of Auguft 1736
aged 47 years.

In 1984 a new headstone
replaced the badly weathered
stone on musician John
Kellner's grave.

The tomb also contains the body of his six year old son, another Thomas, who died in the same year.

In St Catherine, Bearwood, is a memorial to another carpenter, Isaac Gleed, who died in 1891, having worked at Bearwood House for forty-six years. Bearwood was the largest of the new country houses built in Berkshire in the nineteenth century. The owner was John Walter III. Isaac Gleed must have helped to build the house and continued to work there until his retirement. His epitaph reads:

In Loving Memory
of
ISAAC GLEED
WHO DIED NOVEMBER 28th 1891
IN HIS 82nd YEAR
HAVING LIVED AND WORKED 46 YEARS
AS CARPENTER AT BEARWOOD.

Musicians are commemorated in many churchyards in Berkshire. Henry Picks' gravestone is partly hidden under a mass of tangled undergrowth in a corner of St Peter and St Andrew's churchyard, Old Windsor. His epitaph reads:

To the Memory
OF MR HENRY PICK
Late of Her Majesty's
Band of Muficians
Who Died on the
2lft. of March/1810.

However, John Robert Kellners' memorial stands out clearly in St Andrew's churchyard, Clewer, for this gravestone replaced the old, badly weathered one and was paid for in 1984 by the West German Ambassador in London to celebrate the 500th Anniversary of Martin Luthers' birth – for Kellner was a descendent of Martin Luther.

The Kellners were a family of court musicians. One was an oboe player in Queen Charlottes' orchestra. Two others are described in Clewer church registers as 'Musicians to his Majesty'. One of them, Ernest Augustus, was an infant prodigy and played a Handel concerto before the Royal Family at the age of five. He was credited with more than 100 compositions and died in 1839 of a 'decline'.

Kellners' epitaph reads:

HERE LIES
JOHN ROBERT KELLNER
WHO DIED IN WINDSOR
APRIL 19TH 1870
AGED 60 YEARS
AND ALSO MARY ANN ELIZABETH
KELLNER
HIS SISTER
THE LAST LINEAL DESCENDANT
OF THE ENGLISH BRANCH OF MARTIN
LUTHER'S FAMILY
DIED AUGUST 11th 1884
IN HER 43rd YEAR.

A more modern gravestone for a musician can also be found in the same churchyard, and it seemed surprising that after extensive research, no further details can be found about

The grave of Eton music master Mark Clapshaw.

Mark Boyne Clapshaw, considering the words on the stone.

IN LOVING MEMORY OF
MARK BOYNE CLAPSHAW
ASSISTANT MUSIC MASTER
ETON COLLEGE
AT REST 9 JULY 1919
AGED 56
HE WAS LOVED & HONOURED
AND WILL NOT BE FORGOTTEN.

Travelling by coach was a dangerous business in the 18th century, often involving great hardship both for the passengers and coachmen. Sometimes coaches became wedged in snowdrifts and passengers froze to death, or they were swept away by floods. Even if passengers did arrive safely, they often found the journey slow and tiring.

The fastest conveyances were the mail coaches, which began replacing the postboys on horseback along the main post roads in 1784. James

James Murray's gravestone.

Charles Tull's gravestone.

Murray was a coachman travelling from London to Bath through Speen and would have had no easy task driving along the rutted roads in all weathers, pleasing his passengers, being on the alert for possible attacks from highwaymen, and above all satisfying his employers and inkeepers to keep to a scheduled timetable. Perhaps his death at the early age of forty six was a welcome release from such a hard working life.

James Murrays' gravestone is in the churchyard of St Mary the Virgin, Speen, in an isolated and quiet area where sheep nibble the grass around the aged tombstones.

In memory of
JAMES MURRAY
(late Bath Coachman)
who died 26th May 1796
Aged 46 Years.
Tho while on earth I did remain
I was reproach and fcorn by men,
But now am numbered

with the faints
And saf'd of all my long complaints.

The life of a lock-keeper was slower-paced, but carried as many responsibilities. The Thames Conservancy usually employed retired petty officers to take charge of their locks, men with an observant eye, and the experience and character nurtured by naval service to carry out the responsibilities.

It is not known whether Charles Tull was a naval man, but he was lock keeper of Romney Lock for thirty seven years and throughout that time would have had to work eighteen to twenty hours a day during the summer months, be polite, forebearing, active, resolute and resourceful.

Death by drowning was much more of a reality for lock-keepers and their families in the 1800s, than it is today. A catalogue of deaths by drowning occurred from 1869 – the Hurley lock-keeper and then his wife had a narrow escape owing to the dilapidated state of the lock-side; the Whitchurch keeper and his son were both lost in 1871; the Pinkhill keeper drowned in 1881; both Abingdon and Caversham keepers were lost in 1883; the Shiplake keeper drowned in 1890 and in December of that year the Hambledon keeper also drowned.

Many lock keepers were real characters and some performed police duties as water baliffs, patrolling the towpath, and were officers of the Thames Angling Preservation Society.

Charles Tull must have been a well-respected lock-keeper and his gravestone lying slightly askew in the churchyard is a pleasing epitaph to his memory:

SACRED

TO

THE MEMORY OF

CHARLES TULL

LOCK KEEPER OF ROMNEY LOCK

WINDSOR, FOR UPWARDS OF 37 YEARS.

DIED 31ST MARCH 1868

AGED 67 YEARS. THIS MEMORY WAS

PLACED HERE BY SEVERAL OF HIS

FRIENDS BY WHOM HE WAS MUCH

RESPECTED.

Finally in this section are servants. In the eighteenth and nineteenth centuries their work must often have been unbearable drudgery over long hours, yet many country folk preferred service to farm labouring or some other menial work. Sometimes they stayed with the same family for their whole lives, starting when they were children and remaining until they were too old to work any more. Some masters paid for handsome monuments for their servants. This was so in the case of Hannah Cottingham who was a servant for forty five years to John Crewe's family who lived at Woolhampton. Her double headstone with a long and fine epitaph can be seen in the churchyard of St Peter:

Under this ftone lies the Remains of
HANNAH COTTINGHAM,
forty-five Years
Servant to the late John Crewe
Efq. of Woolhampton Houfe and to his
widow and heirs, in which capacity
fhe was to the laft moment of her
Exiftence, a patern of fidelity, zeal
and honefty. She was for feveral
Years afflicted with the dropfy and
after having repeatedly
endured the operations rendered
necefsary by it with Chriftian
fortitude/and refignation.
She concluded her useful
Life on the 14th of April 1811 in the
73rd Year of her Age.
To her merits as a servant fhe united
a charitable difpofition which in
every ftation of Life is the brighteft
ornament of human nature and in the
final diftribution of the little
property her honeft induftry pro-
duced. She devoted a large portion
of its amounts to the benefit of the

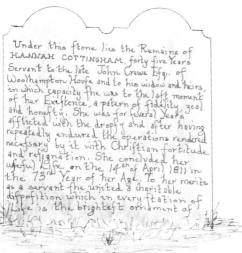

Under this stone lies the Remains of
HANNAH COTTINGHAM, forty five Years
Servant to the late John Crewe Esq. of
Woolhampton House and to his widow and heirs,
in which capacity she was to the last moment
of her Existence, a pattern of fidelity, zeal
and honesty. She was for several Years
afflicted with the dropsy and after having
repeatedly endured the operations rendered
necessary by it with Christian fortitude
and resignation. She concluded her
useful Life on the 14th of April 1811 in
the 73d Year of her Age. To her merits
as a servant she united a charitable
disposition which in every station of
Life is the brightest ornament of

Hannah Cottingham.

poor. The Grandchildren and surviving heirs of the said JOHN CREWE Esq., having witnessed from their early childhood the excellent qualities of this good and faithful Servant feel a melancholy pleasure in thus recording them. They will meet their reward.

To have been a servant and remembered with such love and respect is a wonderful accolade, and perhaps to have been a Maid of Honour and Woman of the Bedchamber to Queen Victoria was equally worth remembering. Certainly the memorial to The Honourable Emily Sarah Cathcart, situated close to the walls of St Michael's Church, Sunninghill, in pink marble, is a very fine example. Queen Victoria demanded impeccable discretion in the conduct of all her servants. They had to conform to the rules of conduct she established for her Household. It was well-known, for instance, that she did not approve of any of its younger members, of either sex, getting married. The Maids of Honour, in fact, had never been allowed to receive any men, even brothers, in their own rooms, and they had had to entertain them as best they could in the waiting room downstairs.

The more senior servants, such as the resident Bedchamber Woman, received a salary of £300 a year. At that time it was an excellent salary, especially as the housekeeper received only £112 a year; a Mistress of the Robes received £500. So Emily Cathcart would not only have received a good salary, but would also have had many servants to assist her, including linen women who were paid £60 a year.

The family tomb of the Cathcarts states that the Emily was born on November 29, 1834, and died on February 16, 1917

Other epitaphs to tradespeople and professionals

Here lyeth body of
JAMES FRANCKLIN
Joynery Sitison of London
who departed this life

ye 16 of February. An Dm
1704.   J.F.1704.
St James, Finchampstead

In Memory of FABIAN WIGGINS,
Cordmaker and Citizen of London
who died Dec Ye 5th AD 1737.
Aged 49 year.
Reader the mournful object
here you see
May serve to mind us of eternity
... either soon or late we all
must come
Mould or to dust and sink
into the tomb.
St Mary, Cholsey

In memory of William Coleman, who
died Oct.26th 1852 aged 80 years. A
working shoemaker in occupation for
more than 60 years he spent all his
leisure hours in visiting the sick and
dying he delighted to testify the
gospel of the grace of God unto all
men and to many did the Lord seem
to bless his labours of faithfulness
and love and they that are wise shall
shine as the brightness of the firma-
ment and they that turn many to
righteousness as the stars for ever
and ever.
St Giles, Reading

In Memory of
THOMAS CHAMBERS
who died suddenly on his way
to Church, Sunday evening
July 21 1861, aged

64 years, after
faithfully fulfilling the
office of Sexton, also
Sergeant atMace and other
offices under the Corporation
for 31 years.
O ask thyself as moments fly
Am I myself prepared to die.
All Saints, Wokingham

In humble hope of a joyful
resurrection
Here rest the mortal remains of
Richard Sherwood Esq.,
for many years an eminent surgeon
at Reading.
He died at Speen Hill July 31. 1863
aged 80 years.
Esteemed and respected in life and in
death lamented.
I know that my redeemer liveth.
St Mary the Virgin, Purley

WRITERS

IN THE eighteenth century the growth of trade and commerce, combined with better transport, brought wealth and a higher standard of living to more people. Intellectual and social life were stimulated by the spread of education and by the growing volume of reading matter put out by the presses.

Newspapers and books became extremely popular and local papers became an important part of the link between towns and outlying villages, containing advertisements giving information about local events.

People read books about travel, philosophy, science and agriculture; they read poetry and novels and began collections for their own libraries. By the end of the century circulating libraries made books more accessible to everyone.

John Newbery was a figure of great literary interest in the eighteenth century. He was born into a farming family, but found his way into journalism at Reading, and was the first bookseller who made the issue of books especially for children a business of any importance. He is remembered as the publisher of *Goody Two Shoes*. He was an author of some repute and many thought that he had written *Goody Two Shoes* himself, but certainly *The Vicar of Wakefield* was his own work.

He was a great friend of Oliver Goldsmith and often helped him financially for the Irish doctor made a lot of money but was not very good at managing it.

John Newbery died on December 22, 1767, aged fifty four and is buried in the churchyard of Waltham St Lawrence. In his Will dated 1763 he states:

'ffirst I desire I may be buried as private as possible in the Church Yard of the parish of Lawrence Waltham near my late ffather and mother and in the daytime if it be convenient and I desire that my Corps may be carried from the Hearse to the grave by six very poor men of the said parish, and that six other poor old men of the said parish do support the pall and that each and every one of them be paid half a guinea for their trouble and attendance....'

The epitaph on his tombstone reads:

John Newbery's tombstone.

Here lieth the Body of
JOHN NEWBERY OF
St Paul's Churchyard, London
Bookſeller
who died December 22,1767
Aged 54 Years.
Writer of Children's Stories
Publisher and friend of
OLIVER GOLDSMITH
and
Dr. SAMUEL JOHNSON.

A literary man of some distinction is buried in St James's churchyard, Barkham. He was the Reverend Peter Hampson Ditchfield, Rector of Barkham for forty four years and the author of more than 100 books on history, village life and ecclesastical matters.

He was a Lancashire man who became a priest in 1878 and was first appointed to a curacy in Sandhurst, two years later moving to Christ Church, Reading. In 1886 he was appointed Rector of Barkham. This was an ideal parish for Ditchfield, for it allowed him time to write. *The History of Berkshire, Bygone Berkshire; Handbook of Gothic Architecture* and *Cathedrals of Great Britain* were just some of his output, apart from contributions to periodical publications on history, archaeology, topography, architecture, village life and old country life.

When Ditchfield died the church was not big enough to accommodate all the people who wished to attend the funeral and pay a last tribute to a man of learning and charming personality.

The Rector was laid to rest in a grave lined with ferns, under the shadow of the south wall of his church, and the ground around the grave was a sea of flowers and wreaths. The epitaph on his white stone cross reads:

SACRED
TO THE MEMORY OF
MY HUSBAND
PETER HAMPSON DITCHFIELD, M.A.,
44 YEARS THE DEARLY LOVED
RECTOR OF THIS PARISH
DIED SEPT. 23rd 1930
AGED 76 YEARS.

One Berkshire author who deserves a mention is Kenneth Grahame, simply because when he died he was actually buried in the churchyard of St James the Less, Pangbourne, but was later moved to Holywell Cemetery, Oxford.

Kenneth Grahame, famous for the much loved *Wind in the Willows,* lived in Church Cottage at Pangbourne. When he died in 1932 his funeral at St James the Less was described in *The Times* of July 11: *'The church was a marvellous sight – a blaze of glorious colour and sunshine – with masses of flowers, delphiniums, and roses and willows gathered from the river that morning. And perhaps the most touching thing of all were the flowers sent by chil-*

dren from all over the country with cards attached in a childish scrawl saying how much they loved him. The grave was lined with thousands of sweet peas and the scent was unforgettable.'

Another writer who in a sense has been lost to Berkshire is Agatha Christie, for she lies in the churchyard at St Mary's Cholsey, which is now in Oxfordshire, but which was once in Berkshire.

Agatha Christie, the Queen of Crime, was the most widely published author of all time, outsold only by the Bible and Shakespeare. Agatha Miller was born on September 15, 1890, in Torquay, and in 1914 she married Archibald Christie. In 1920 her first book *The Mysterious Affair at Styles* was published, by Bodley Head, having been rejected by six other publishers.

A few months after publication of *The Murder of Roger Ackroyd*, she disappeared. The mystery writer was suddenly headline news, her name known throughout the country. Some said that it was a publicity stunt and indeed it did have a considerable effect on the sales of her books, but more likely she escaped from the effects of a marriage that had gone badly wrong and needed to be on her own. Then suddenly, just before Christmas 1926, she was found staying at The Hydropathic Hotel in Harrogate, suffering from loss of

The Queen of Crime, Agatha Christie, is buried here with her husband Max.

memory. Whatever the real story, a divorce followed soon afterwards.

The year 1930 was a momentous one both for Agatha Christie and for the house of Collins, her publisher. In September she married the archaeologist Max Mallowan and in the same year Collins published *Murder at the Vicarage*. This was the first book under a new six-book contract in which Miss Jane Marple was introduced.

Her work has been translated into forty four languages. In 1947 Queen Mary, who was a Christie fan, asked her to attempt a radio play. The Queen and the radio audience seemed to like the result and Christie decided to turn it into a stage play. It was called *The Mousetrap* and was produced at the Ambassadors Theatre in 1952. It has been running in the West End ever since.

Ten years before she died Agatha Christie, who had been made a Dame of the British Empire, chose the site at St Mary's churchyard, Cholsey, for her burial, as well as choosing the lines on the tombstone, which are from Spenser's *The Faerie Queen.*

In Memoriam
AGATHA MARY CLARISSA
MALLOWAN
DBE
Agatha Christie. Author & Playwright
BORN *15th* SEPT.R. *1890.*
DIED *12th* JAN.Y. *1976*
Sleepe after toyle,
port, after stormie seas
Ease after war,
death after life does greatly please.
ALSO HER HUSBAND
MAX EDGAR LUCIEN
MALLOWAN
Archealogist & Orientalist
Membre de Institut de France.
BORN *6th* MAY *1904.*
DIED *19th* AUG.T. *1978*

In the churchyard at All Saints, Swallowfield, lies Mary Mitford, a prolific nineteenth century writer. Of her home county she wrote: '. . . nor could a prettier county be found for our walk than this shady and yet sunny Berkshire, where the scenery, without rising into grandeur or breaking into wildness, is so peaceful, so cheerful, so varied, and so thoroughly English.'

Mary Mitford was born on December 16, 1786, and she was only ten when she chose the number 2224 – numerals that added up to her age – for her father's lottery number. The family won £20,000, an absolute fortune in those days.

Her father built Reading House with some of the money, and unfortunately took up gambling with the rest. By 1820, all the money had been spent. Mary, in her early thirties, took refuge in a labourer's cottage in the village of Three Mile Cross. She supported her ailing mother and her incorrigible father for more than thirty years on the proceeds of her literary labours.

At first she decided to be a dramatist. She wrote four plays which were performed at Drury Lane and Covent Garden, and earned hundreds of pounds from them.

She then began writing for *The Lady,* which at that time was quite obscure. The circulation shot up after a few issues containing her work and although her life was not easy and she had to spend eight to twelve hours a day at her desk, she managed to earn a regular income from her pen.

Mary's accounts of village life were soon published in book form, called *Our Village*, which is still available in Berkshire book shops and libraries today.

She continued to write after her parents' deaths but was crippled by rheumatism and neuralgia. Her last years were a sad story of helpless invalidism. Some financial help had come from a Civil List pension of £100 a year and later, after her fathers' death, by a fund raised in compassion by many of her friends.

The cottage at Three Mile Cross had fallen into disrepair and she was given sanctuary in a cottage in the village of Swallowfield by Lady Russell of Swallowfield Park, a devoted friend.

A cross marks the grave of sad Mary Mitford.

A carriage accident when she was flung out on the road whilst visiting Lady Russell left her partially paralysed for the last two years of her life.

Mary Mitford died on January 10, 1855, and was buried close to the railings separating Swallowfield Park from the churchyard of All Saints.

Another writer who loved his

The last resting place of writer Robert Gibbings.

county and inspired all who read his work was Robert John Gibbings. One of his books, *Sweet Thames Run Softly*, can, like Mary Mitfords' book, still be obtained from the library. Anyone who takes the time to delve into it will be drawn down to the banks of the Thames running through Berkshire and Old Berkshire, to listen and linger as the writer did when it was published back in 1940.

Robert Gibbings, born in 1889, was an author, book designer and wood-engraver. He served in Gallipoli in 1915, was shot through the throat and invalided out of the Army. Between 1924 and 1933, he was proprietor of The Golden

Cockerel Press, which produced seventy two volumes, nineteen of which were illustrated by Gibbings.

He wrote many travel books, but his biggest success was *Sweet Thames Runs Softly* which enjoyed great success. In his book Gibbings talks about collecting yellow lichen from tombstones in the churchyards he wandered through. From this lichen he made a dye which made his tie purple. He felt it was not sacriligeous to use the lichen in that way. He told how having made the dye, he wore the tie and 'accepted the subsequent admiration with humility'.

Robert Gibbings died in 1958 in Oxford, three months after the publication of his last book, *Till I End My Song*, another book about the Thames. He is buried in the churchyard at St Mary Virgin, Long Wittenham, under a simple headstone that states his name with a feather quill pen underneath and his dates.

A sombre grey slate memorial for the author Christopher Reynolds Stone can be found in Eton College churchyard. Born in 1882, he was joint founder of the *The Gramophone* publication and the author of many novels – *Scars, Valley of Indecision* and *Rigour of the Game* were some of his titles, and there were many books about Eton and the surrounding area.

Stone was the first British 'disc jockey' for 2LO Radio in the 1920s.

The distinctive headstone for Christopher Stone.

He had a Friday lunchtime programme. He died on May 22, 1965. His memorial stone reads:

> *Christopher Reynolds*
> STONE
> DSO MG,
> *devoted husband of*
> *Alyce Wilson Chinnery,*
> *who broadcast his love of music*
> *to millions*
> *lies here within sight of*
> *his birthplace.*
> *1882-1965.*

Of the authors who write under

pseudonyms, two such are buried in Berkshire.

Edward William Cuming, born in 1862, was an author and journalist who wrote some books under his own name – *British Sport, Past and Present* (1909), *A Fox-hunting Anthology* (1928), *In the Shadow of the Pagoda* (1893).

Under the name Evelyn Tempest he wrote *The Doubts of Diana* (1911), *Poor Emma!* (1911) and *A Rogue's March* (1913).

Cuming died in 1941 and is buried in the churchyard of St Peter and St Paul, Appleford.

The name Eric Arthur Blair might not ring a bell with most people, but change it to George Orwell and there are few who have not read or heard of him

Orwell was born into a poor, but proud middle-class family. Sent to a private school, he won a scholarship to Eton where his snobbish upbringing and the uneasiness he felt living with boys richer than himself, gave him a distaste for middle-class values.

He served in the Burma Police for five years until 1927 and then tried to appease his sense of guilt by living in the utmost destitution for eighteen months when he wrote *Down and Out in London and Paris.*

At the height of the Depression in the 1930s, the publishers Gollancz commissioned Orwell to make a per-

Eric Arthur Blair, alias George Orwell, lies here.

sonal investigation of conditions in the north of England. By the time his results were published in a book called *The Road to Wigan Pier* in 1937, he was fighting for the Republicans in Spain where he was wounded.

When World War Two started Orwell was rejected for the army on medical grounds and worked for the Indian service of the BBC. Then in 1945 came the novel *Animal Farm -*

a satire on Stalinism; 4,500 copies were published, and the edition was sold out in two weeks. After the war he wrote his most famous book, *1984,* a vision of a world ruled by dictatorships taken to an extreme.

Orwell became literary editor of *The Tribune* for two years from 1943 to 1945, but aged only forty seven he died of a lung haemorrhage in January, 1950.

His burial was arranged by David Astor of *The Observer*, after Orwell had expressed an objection in his will to cremation. Certainly his gravestone with the simple epitaph almost obscured by two rose bushes reflects the character and humility of the writer.

HERE LIES

ERIC ARTHUR BLAIR

BORN JUNE 25th 1903

DIED JANUARY 21st 1950.

There are quite a few poets buried in the county of Berkshire, whose graves can be visited, but Sir Benjamin Rudyerd, who was both poet and politician, is buried close to his house in the graveyard of a vanished church in West Woodhay.

Although his grave and the epitaph he composed himself cannot now be seen,he is remembered as one of the most eloquent and peaceful of men who lived in an age of turbulence and unhappiness.

Born on the December 26, 1572, Rudyerd was educated at Winchester School and went to St John's College, Oxford. On April 18, 1600, he was admitted to the Inner Temple a.nd in October of that same year called to the Bar.

His poems, although not printed until after his death, gained Rudyerd a considerable reputation as a poet, and he was also accepted as a critic of poetry. He associated with Ben Johnson who wrote an epigram addressed to Rudyerd praising his virtues, his friendship and his 'learned muse'.

His political career began in 1620 when he was returned to Parliament for the borough of Portsmouth; he was well known for his speeches which were said to combine zeal for the cause of the elector with a desire to propitiate the king!

After many years in Parliament Rudyerd supported the Presbyterians in 1648, in urging meetings with the King, and was arrested and imprisoned for some hours.

For the last ten years of his life until his death in 1658, Rudyerd took no further part in public affairs, and died at his house in West Woodhay on the May 31, aged eighty six.

A memorial for a poet laureate can be found in the churchyard of St Peter and St Paul, Yattendon. Robert Bridges, born in 1844, was poet laureate for seventeen years until his death in 1930. As well as writing poetry he produced several critical

Laurence Binyon, remembered for his elegant poetry.

essays, but his most famous philosophical poem, *The Testament of Beauty*, was written only a year before he died.

In 1898 Robert Bridges put up a churchyard cross to mark the grave of his mother, Harriet Molesworth. His own ashes were buried nearby.

In the churchyard of St Mary, Aldworth, is the grave of Laurence Binyon, a long time friend of Robert Bridges. Binyon was born in 1869 and for forty years worked as assistant keeper in the Department of Oriental Prints and Drawings in the British Museum. It is for his volumes of poetry that he is remembered and in particular the poem *To the Fallen*, which was written for Armistice Day November 11, 1918, and was set to music by Elgar. This poem includes the lines:

'They shall grow not old, as we that are left grow old:
Age shall not weary them, nor the years condemn.
At the going down of the sun and in the morning
We will remember them.'

Laurence Binyon died in a Reading nursing home in 1943, following an operation for appendicitis. His memorial in the churchyard at Aldworth lies flat along the ground in front of a hedge with the simple epitaph of:

LAURENCE BINYON
1869 - 1943
AND CICELY HIS WIFE
1876 - 1962.

MISCELLANEOUS

IN PARISH churches the earliest tombs are those from the twelfth century. These were often stone slabs commemorating churchmen or those who were wealthy enough to be buried inside the church. Clergymen were often interred facing west, the idea being that when the final day of judgement came, everyone would rise up facing Jerusalem and all clerics would be in a natural position to address their congregations.

Throughout the Middle Ages the poor were very often buried in the churchyards without memorials, one on top of another, over the centuries.

The oldest graves face the south as it was desirable to avoid the church's shadow falling across them. It was said that the Devil lurked among the shadows and was always supposed to enter a churchyard from the north; thus this side of the churchyard was often reserved for suicides and murderers.

At one time murders were common in Berkshire. Before the suspect could be executed and buried in the north side of the churchyard he was taken with the corpse up into the church tower, the idea being, that if the person was guilty the corpse would bleed when touched by him or her.

On one occasion, this weird and horrible test was performed in Brimton church tower, but in this case was unsuccessful, the reason being, said the old man who told the story, that the corpse had been dead too long.

John Carter was guilty of arson and is buried in the churchyard of St Michael and All Angels, Lambourn. His epitaph reads:

Here
lies the body
of JOHN CARTER
of this parish, labourer
Who in the defiance of the laws
of God and man
wilfully and maliciously
set fire in two places
to the town of Lambourne
on the 30th years of his age
on the 16th day of March, 1853
having desired that his body
might be interred here as a
warning to his companions
and others who may hereafter
read this memorial to his
untimely end.
The wages of sin is death
Repent and turns yourselves from
all your transgressions and so
iniquity shall not be your ruin.

Did John Carter express this wish or was this put on his headstone as a warning to others?

Until the early nineteenth century churchyards were sometimes cleared and the bones stored in charnel houses. In some places the dead were buried on top of older graves. This custom raised the level of old churchyards several feet above the ground outside the church and moats were often dug surrounding the church walls because of the drainage problems caused by these burials.

This was certainly the case at St Andrews, Sonning. Around 1858 an addition was added to the churchyard from land known as Bone Orchard. There is no reason to suppose that Bone Orchard formed part of the original churchyard, but quantities of human skulls and bones, as well as bones of animals were found.

Some were buried so tightly together it was presumed that it could once have been a Saxon burial place of a battlefield, or that the bones had been collected from elsewhere and taken for burial to Bone Orchard.

As it was known that there was always a preference to be buried on the south side of the church, it could often be that the north would remain deserted. In St Andrews it was discovered during restoration work that the burials on the south side had been so excessive that they had to remove at least two feet of earth which had accumulated against the church wall, and lower the whole of the south part of the churchyard. The bones were collected and buried in pits under the gravel walk.

During the work ancient tiles were discovered; they must have been cast out of the church when the pavement was removed at different times to make room for vaults.

Cemeteries on the outskirts of towns solved the problem of overcrowding in the churchyards. Liverpool led the way by opening the first cemetery in 1825. This was fine until the ever increasing population caused the same problem all over again, thus in the 1880s crematoria appeared on the scene.

In 1660 there was a major revolution in grave clothes, indirectly leading to the idea of undertaking as a distinct trade. In this year an Act decreed that all persons had to be buried in shifts, shrouds and winding sheets made of woollen material rather than linen, and free from 'Flax, Hemp, Silk, Hair, Gold or Silver, or other than that what is made of Sheeps Wooll only'.

Not everyone was willing to abide by this Act so it had to be strengthened in 1678 by another, this time imposing a fine on all defaulters.

The Act further instructed that the curate of every parish should keep a register, provided at the expense of the parish, into which all burials had to be entered. Sometimes this led to delay in burial, although there was a waiver for death by plague.

Some parishioners did not wait until their deaths. Young brides, especially in remote country areas, included such items in their trousseaux, either buying them ready-made or having them made. They would also have had one or two smaller versions made, for infant mortality was high.

Many people saved for their burials, even depriving themselves of meals so that a funeral could be paid for. People who could not afford the fees had to make do with a pauper's burial, often common for young children right up until the twentieth century. A pauper's burial was paid for by the parish from funds generated from charities.

Many people were buried in shrouds only, although there was a 'parish coffin' kept in the church which was used over and over again for the funerals of poor people.

By 1830, with the repeal of the Act for Burial in Woollen, other materials such as calico, cambric, cashmere, flannel, linen, muslin, poplin, satin, serge and silk were being used. Sometimes these were used to line the coffin as well.

Those who died in an outlying part of the parish had to have their funeral carefully planned so that parish boundaries were not tres-

The headstone of Ellen Smallbone in the churchyard at St James, Finchampstead.

passed by the body. Sometimes streams had to be forded and fields of crops walked through in order to avoid straying across a boundary.

During the eighteenth century the horse-drawn hearse was used, sometimes with enormous pomp depending upon the importance of the person being buried.

However, in most villages and small towns through the 1800s and into the 1900s, the wheeled bier was the usual conveyance from home to church to graveside. From 1850 coffins were allowed to be transported by rail and most stations had their own coffin trolleys. The first motorised hearse appeared in 1900.

The earliest churchyard gravestones were very simple, just a stone at the head of the grave and a smaller one at the foot. They would sometimes be only two feet high, but gradually they got bigger and more varied in design.

Grave spaces in churchyards were measured in yards and feet. Graves occupied up to eight feet by two feet, and slabs covering brick lined vaults were eight feet by four feet.

Headstones and footstones ranged through the centuries from those with semi-circular or contoured heads to large rectangular slabs which, if placed upright, served as headstones, and if laid flat, were called ledgers.

These slabs became popular during the period when body snatchers were at work stealing corpses for medical research. The grave robbers found a ledger tomb too difficult to lift up and they moved elsewhere.

In the eighteenth century some tombs took on a classical Roman look with stone pedestals in the shapes of urns. These were sometimes carved with a draped cloth to portray mourning. Often on tombs containing whole families masons would carve skulls for faces, as a sign that children and perhaps grandchildren died before their parents.

Most gravestones are made of stone and until a century or so ago, masons had to use rocks in their own locality, very often from the same quarry which provided the stone for the parish church.

Stratfield Mortimer parish church contains what is probably the oldest tombstone in Berkshire. It is the stone cover, over six feet long, of a Saxon tomb made in the half century before the Conquest. Round it in Saxon lettering with Roman capitals, runs an inscription which reads:

On the eighth before the Kalends of October Aegelward son of Kypping was laid in this place. Blessed be the man who prays for his soul.
Toki wrote me.

Toki was a courtier of King Canute. Kypping held two manors in Berkshire and it is believed that the stone covered the body of an ealdorman of Hampshire who made friends with invading Danes after the declaration of peace.

For generations his tombstone lay buried under the tower of the old church, but it now stands against the south wall of the chancel of St Mary.

There were occasional metal monuments using lead or iron as seen in St Nicholas Parish churchyard, Hurst, and St Mary's, Hampstead Norreys. And sometimes wood was used, but many of the old wooden crosses seen in Berkshire churchyards have rotted so badly that the inscription is unreadable and all or most of the actual cross has disappeared. One exception is the 'rail' in the churchyard at St Lawrence, Reading, and another is a post close to the north side of the churchyard at St James, Ruscombe, which reads:

In ever present memory
of our brother James Gwynne Verey
this water supply is given by his sisters
August 31st 1933.

Some of the earliest tombstones had very simple lettering – as this one in St Mary's, Reading:

1791. July 21.
William Randall, buried.

The masons who carved the gravestones were often more skilled at country crafts than definite lettering and many had to supply the verses. Some came from a book of printed epitaphs but many were composed especially for the death, depicting his or her character and mode of death. An example is that at St Mary's, Hampstead Norreys, dated August 20, 1722:

Richard, son of Luke and
Elizabeth Spicer, aged 21
A sincere youth of solid
judgement and no meddler
in other people's concerns,
ideoque magis lugendus
(and therefore the more to be
lamented or bewailed).

An epitaph in Harwell church is for John Jennings who died in 1599, leaving six sons and five daughters:

Good wife and children agree
Serve God and come to mee.

The stonemason would also have had to decide about the letters; there were several versions for some of them, like the long and the short *s*.

In the eighteenth century Roman lettering was very popular and stonemasons were most probably able to use their own iniative as to how decorative each letter could be.

The Victorian period produced many magnificent memorials. No longer did the deceased die but instead 'fell asleep'. The prevailing epitaph of our forefathers was:

Free from malice, void of pride,
So he lived, and so he died.

Many simple verses can be seen again and again in the churchyards of this county:

God's finger touch'd him
and he slept.

She is not dead, but sleepeth.

A Gentleman, a scholar
and an Honest man.

When I am laid in the green
churchyard say not that she did
well or ill, only she did her best.

To live in the hearts of those
we love is not to die.

There were obviously fashions in epitaphs which varied according to the class of the buried person or the age he or she died. Religious beliefs dictated 'God's will' being mentioned often and puns were occasionally used. When a man named Thomas Little, who owned a large estate in Bray, died, his friends wrote in his epitaph:

Although thou called were
Littill by thy name,
In with thy mind and Godlyness
full great yet was in fame,
Yet where thou wast before but
great, through Virtue sewre,
Thou greater now, doest rest in
heaven, for ever to endure.

The hour-glass was often referred to in epitaphs, particularly in times when clocks were a rarity. If the hour-glass had two wings, one of a bird indicating day, and the other a bat for night – this was to show the passing of time. Examples can be seen in Swallowfield churchyard.

Sometimes wings would appear on monuments and this was meant to show the soul of the dead person flying up to Heaven. Complete angels were carved on tombs as country masons tried to copy their town counterparts, depicting winged soul cherubs on the fashionable tombstones of the wealthy.

Consumption was once a common cause of death. Seen in nearly every churchyard in Berkshire is this well used epitaph:

The pale consumption gave
the final blow
The stroke was fatal but
the effect was slow
With wasting pain I sorely
was oppressed
Till God was pleased by death
to give me rest.

Plagues such as cholera were common right into the last century. When this happened it was usual to bury the victims all together in an unused part of the churchyard. Smallpox in some ways resembled the feared plague in that one isolated community could be completely free of it, whilst another, through a chance intruder, might be totally wiped out.

Other diseases such as leprosy, syphilis, measles and typhus, claimed many lives, as did the scourges of today, heart disease and cancer. A floor tablet in St James the Less, Pangbourne, is perhaps the first recorded evidence of a mastectomy. The tablet is for Jane Robinson, wife of Thomas Robinson 'Chiefe Prothonotary of H.M. Court of Common Pleas' who died at Bere Court:

...in ye 49 yeare of her age by cancer in her breast which she suffered with an invincible patience to be cut of, and survived onely 6 months after, dyed on ye 22 November, 1665, and was here interred December ye 8th, to whose deare memorie her most indulgent husband hath erected this adjoyning monument.

Quite often people would write their own epitaphs long before they died. Ann Richards, who lived in Compton Beauchamp, and was extremely rich and beautiful, preferred coursing to men and although she received many suitors, stayed single. She loved to course hares with her famously fast greyhounds. She died in 1771 and her epitaph shows she was a woman of character and great humour:

All arts and sciences beside
This hare-brained heroine
did deride.
An utter foe to wedlock's noose,
When poaching men had stopt the
Meuse.
Tattle and tea, she was above it,
And but for form appeared to love it.
At books she laughed, at Pope
and Clarke,
And all her joy was Ashdown Park.
But Ann at length was spied by death,
Who coursed, and
ran her out of breath.

Hannah Deeley, who lived in Wargrave, left instructions to be buried in St Mary's, and wrote:

'My body I commend to the earth to be buried – decent Christian Burial, and desire that there be at my Funeral for the persons attending the same, one leg of Veal and one Gammon of Bacon, with such quantity of Beer as shall be thought necessary by my Executors and I desire to be buried – a plain coffin without one nail in the lid and that I may be carried to the grave by six poor men of the Parish of Wargrave, who are not in the Workhouse, and that six poor widows of the same parish, who are not in the Workhouse, may bear up my pall and that there be given to each of the said men and women,

also to the Clerk of the same parish for the time being, one Gallon Loaf, one Pound of Bacon and one Pound of Cheese.'

At St James, Finchampstead, over the entrance door of the west chapel the inscription *T.H.1590* can be seen. This was for Thomas Harrison who, in his Will of 1602, left legacies for the poor people of Finchampstead, Ockingham, Barkam, Strathfieldse and Swallowfield – *'upon condition that they stay at home and content themselves to receive this my benevolence at their own parishes and not to be troublesome at my buriall. My body to be buried in the Porch of the West Doore of the Parish Church in the place lately by me prepared.'*

At St Mary's, Hampstead Norreys, there are records of different charities set up by parishioners from 1690 to 1958. In 1690 William Emery provided in his will that money should be given for the purchase of five white fustian greatcoats for shepherds or labourers, annually, and the balance to be distributed in sums of 2/6 and 3/- among indigent widows.

In 1811 Ann Cowslad settled the rents of a piece of land and cottages to be distributed among the poor, for food, clothes and fuel. In the early twentieth century it was mostly given as blue serge pettitcoats.

In 1843, the Reverend James Reed, a former vicar, left £100 to be invested to provide annually a substantial greatcoat for a labourer of good character.

In 1958, all these charities were amalgamated and the money has been distributed since in the form of coal and grocery vouchers.

Yew trees feature prominently in any history of a churchyard and Berkshire has its fair share of famous specimens. Only recently it was discovered that the yew in the churchyard of St Mary the Virgin, White Waltham, is at least 1,600 years old, and still growing.

Waltham St Lawrence has a wonderful old yew tree said to have been planted in 1635. It completely dominates the front of the church, forming a lychgate of its own with huge curving trunks resting along the ground and protruding over the churchyard walls. It is supported by posts that have become branches themselves, weathered over time by rain and wind.

Only a stump remains of an old yew tree in St Clement's churchyard, Ashampstead, but it is built into the wall of the north-west corner of the church. Tradition says that under this tree the Gospel was first preached, long before the church was built and the builders incorporated it into the wall. It is a nice belief.

One of the most famous yew trees in Berkshire is in St Mary's churchyard, Aldworth. For the people of Aldworth it was a tragic event when a storm blew down their 1,000 year

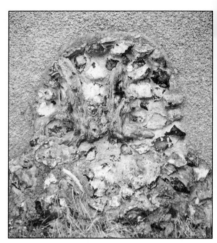

The remains of a yew stump built into the church wall at St Clement's, Ashampstead.

old tree, reducing it from a forty foot beauty to a six foot fragment – but even this is impressive. It was probably this tree that Tennyson mentioned in his poem *In Memorium*. Tennyson lived near Hindhead, but he had fond memories of Aldworth and even named his house after it.

Old Yew, which graspest at the stones
That name the under-lying dead,
Thy fibres net the dreamless head,
Thy roots are wrapt about the bones.

Stone crosses are probably as common in Berkshire churchyards as yew trees, but the crosses seen in St Andrew's churchyard, Clewer, are unusual in their design and history.

Each square holds a different Christian name belonging to a Sister of St John the Baptist Order, and

Right, the 1,000-year-old storm-stunted yew at Aldworth: Above, nuns' graves at St Andrew's, Clewer.

each cross has a lamb in the middle holding a pennant or gideon. The crosses of Sister Harriet May, Sister Mary, Sister Jane and Sister Margaret Esther are shown in the photograph, but more are to be found hidden away among tall grass and brambles in this charming churchyard.

The Sisterhood was founded by Thomas Thellusson Carter, Rector of Clewer for fifty seven years.

Another unusual cross can be seen at the bottom of St Mary's churchyard, Beenham. This rural churchyard contains some of the most original deeply carved tombstones in the county. Most of them are illegible, but even if the epitaph had not been visible it would have been impossible to overlook the mosaic decorating the stone cross of Anne Elizabeth Pearson, who died at Dresden, November 25, 1870, aged fifty nine.

Miscellaneous epitaphs

To the Memory of
LAURENTIUS BRAAG
a Danish Merchant
born in
the Ifland of St Croix
in the West Indies 21 ft July 1783
and died
as a Prisoner of War on Parade in
Reading
the 3d of Sept. 1808
in the 26th Year of his Age
He lived efteemed and beloved by his
Friends and Countrymen
by whom this Stone
is raifed.
St Mary, Reading

To the memory of
William, son of
William & Mary Foreman
who departed this life
the 30th of Jan. 1804
aged 34 years.
Boast not vain man of
constitution strong
Tho' health and vigour may
thy days prolong.
Tho' I long time could boast
as well as thee
of perfect health & from

diseases free
But death regardless of our
joys and cares
Cut off my life in the full
bloom of years.
St Mary, Longcott

In Memory of Mary Codd,
who anxiously looking for the
Blessed Hope of Jesus Christ,
died July 24.1811 after a short
llness in the 76th Year of her Age.
Such the prospects that arise
To the dying Christians eyes,
Such the glorious Vista Faith
Opens through the shades of death.
Holy Trinity, Cookham

Near this place lyeth the remains
of William Harding who as a member
attended the annual meeting of the
Blewbury Friendly Society
the great number of seventy six times,
He died 24th Nov r 1832
aged 94 Years.
This tablet was kindly erected by his
friends and brother members.
St Andrew, East Hagbourne

God grand that her pardon was
sealed in heaven before
she went home
(No name) St Andrew, East
Hagbourne